P O C K E T S
DOGS

Written by
DAVID TAYLOR

DACHSHUNDS

AFGHAN HOUND
PUPPY

GRAY WOLF

DK PUBLISHING

LONDON, NEW YORK,
MELBOURNE, MUNICH, and DELHI

Project editor Selina Wood
Designer Janet Allis
Senior editor Alastair Dougall
Senior art editor Sarah Crouch
Picture research Sam Ruston
Production Josie Alabaster
US editor Constance M. Robinson

REVISED EDITION
Project editor Steve Setford
Designer Sarah Crouch
Managing editor Linda Esposito
Managing art editor Jane Thomas
DTP designer Siu Yin Ho
Consultant David Alderton
Production Erica Rosen
US editors Margaret Parrish, Christine Heilman

Second American Edition, 2003
Published in the United States by
DK Publishing, Inc., 375 Hudson Street,
New York, New York 10014

03 04 05 06 07 08 10 9 8 7 6 5 4 3 2 1

A Cataloging-in-Publication record for the First American Edition of this book
is available from the Library of Congress.

ISBN 0-7894-9591-0

Color reproduction by Colourscan, Singapore
Printed and bound in Italy by L.E.G.O.

See our complete product line at
www.dk.com

CONTENTS

HOW TO USE THIS BOOK

These pages show you how to use *Pockets: Dogs*. The book is divided into six sections. The main sections consist of information about different breeds of domestic dogs. There is an introductory section at the front of the book and a reference section at the back, as well as a glossary and comprehensive index.

HEADING
The heading describes the overall subject of the page. This page is about Collies.

INTRODUCTION
The introduction provides an overview of the subject. After reading this, you should have a clear idea of what the pages are about.

CORNER CODING
The corners of the main section pages are color-coded to remind you which section you are in.

- HOUNDS AND GUNDOGS
- HERDING AND GUARD DOGS
- TERRIERS
- SPECIAL BREEDS AND TOY DOGS

Corner coding

Heading

Introduction

Annotation

Label

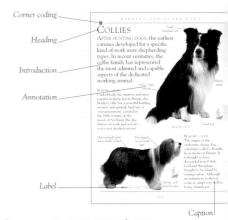

HERDING AND GUARD DOGS

COLLIES

AFTER HUNTING DOGS, the earliest canines developed for a specific kind of work were shepherding types. In recent centuries, the collie family has represented the most admired and capable aspects of the dedicated working animal.

BORDER COLLIE
Undoubtedly the smartest and most popular working dog in Britain, the Border Collie has a powerful herding instinct and aptitude bred into it over generations. Created in the 19th century on the moors of Scotland, this dog thrives on work and activity so it is not an ideal city pet.

BEARDED COLLIE
The origins of this exuberant, shaggy dog, sometimes called a Beardie, lie in medieval Britain. It is thought to have descended from Polish Lowland Sheepdogs brought to Scotland by visiting sailors. Although an industrious worker, it seems to adapt very well to being a family pet.

Small triangular ears

Heavy mane

Dense, short, weather-resistant coat

Small feet

Hair naturally parts down middle of back

Extra length, crested facial hair

Strong, well-boned forelegs

BORDER COLLIE

Caption

CAPTIONS AND ANNOTATIONS
Each illustration carries an explanatory caption. Some also have annotations, in *italics*. These point out the features of an illustration, and often use leader lines.

LABELS
For clarity, some pictures have labels. These give extra information about the picture, or may provide clearer identification.

RUNNING HEADS
These remind you which section you are in. The top of the left-hand page gives the section name, and the top of the right-hand page gives the subject heading.

FACT BOXES
Many pages have fact boxes. These provide at-a-glance information about the subject, such as how many sensory ("sniffing") cells the average dog has.

SIZE INDICATORS
These show the average sizes of the different adult breeds in relation to a 6 ft (1.83 m) human.

Running head　*Size indicator*

Feature box

FEATURE BOXES
These boxes provide additional information. This feature gives details about the Shetland Sheepdog.

REFERENCE SECTION
Where possible, information has been presented in the form of a diagram. This makes data more accessible, and easier to absorb. On these pages, for example, how to give medicine to a dog is shown as an illustration.

INDEX
At the back of the book, there is an index. It lists alphabetically every subject included in the book. By referring to the index, information on particular topics can be found.

INTRODUCTION TO DOGS

WHAT IS A DOG?

THE DOMESTIC DOG, scientific name *Canis familiaris* (from the Latin *canis*, meaning "dog"), is one of 34 living species of canids – meat-eating animals that evolved for the pursuit of prey across open grassland. The dog family ranges from the tiny Fennec Fox to the large Gray Wolf.

Insulating fur

Excellent hearing

Strong jaws and large canine teeth to catch and hold prey

Powerful muscles for speed and endurance

GRAY WOLF

GRAY WOLF
The Gray Wolf, one of two existing wolf species (the other is the endangered Red Wolf of southeastern US), is the ancestor of the domestic dog. It was once the most widespread mammal, apart from humans, outside the tropics.

JACKAL
The jackals of Africa, southeastern Europe, and Asia, have an undeserved bad name. Jackals are good parents to their young and do not scavenge as much as is supposed. Their diet ranges from fruit to small gazelle.

JACKAL

RED FOX

RED FOX
The Red Fox, like all foxes, is a small canid with a slender skull, large ears, and a long, bushy tail. Its coat varies from grayish or rusty red to almost orange. All-black and silvery forms also occur.

Dogs are social animals that adapt to their surroundings easily

PACK INSTINCT

Unlike more specialized carnivores, such as cats, which tend to hunt alone, most canids hunt in packs. Pack members also have a strong instinct to guard pack territory. Such instincts helped domestication, as canids readily adopted a human family as their "pack."

EVOLUTION

About 50 million years ago, in the Eocene epoch, *Miacis*, a small, weasel-like mammal with a well developed brain, was the forefather of all canids, as well as more distantly related carnivores.

By the Miocene epoch, more than 40 ancestors of modern canids had emerged. Tomarctus had the beginnings of modern canine tooth anatomy.

TOMARCTUS

Hesperocyon was a long-bodied, short-limbed canid living in the later Eocene epoch. Fossils have been found in North America.

HESPEROCYON

Miacis had the distinctive teeth of a canid, and also spreading paws, indicating adaptation to life in the trees.

MIACIS

ANCESTORS OF THE DOG

RACOONS   BEARS   WOLVES   WEASELS   CIVETS   HYENAS   CATS

						2
						7
						26
						38
						54

MILLIONS OF YEARS AGO

DOMESTICATION

DOGS WERE FIRST DOMESTICATED from wolves more than 10,000 years ago. Human–dog contact may have evolved as wolves scavenged around human settlements and when wolf cubs were raised as pets. The dog's potential as a reliable guard and excellent hunting companion was soon realized.

Early Asian dogs migrated and interbred with North American wolves

EARLY HUNTING SCENE
Ancient cave paintings depict dogs assisting the hunt, as followers of human "pack" leaders.

The Carolina Dog may be descended from half-wild dogs brought across the Bering Straits by Asian peoples 8,000 years ago

The Chihuahua is possibly the oldest breed on the American continent. It may have been introduced to Mexico by traders from China

MEXICAN HAIRLESS

MEXICAN HAIRLESS
This primitive dog, descended from the Indian wolf, has much in common with the Chinese Crested Dog of mainland Asia, and may be related.

Wolves did not migrate to South America; dogs were brought here by early traders

PHARAOH HOUND
This oldest-recorded breed graces the tombs of ancient Egyptian pharaohs. It was probably a descendant of the Phoenician hound – the Phoenicians traded dogs throughout the Mediterranean.

PHARAOH HOUND

Sheepdogs originated in Europe more than 1,000 years ago

Mastiff-type dogs were domesticated in the Stone Age and later used in battle by the Greeks

The Greyhound is portrayed on 8,000-year-old Mesopotamian pottery

Wolflike dogs similar to spitzes, such as the Elkhound and the Siberian Husky, originated in Arctic regions

DOG OWNERSHIP FACTS

• More than 200 million dogs are kept as pets worldwide.

• North America has the most pet dogs (over 60 million), followed by Russia (21 million) and China (19 million); France has about 11 million; Britain, Japan, and South Africa each have around 7 million.

DINGO
The Dingo was brought to Australia 4,000 years ago. It is now a feral dog (a domesticated dog that has reverted to the wild).

DINGO

BASENJI
The Basenji's roots lie lost in the mists of antiquity. This nonbarking African breed has remained more or less pure for thousands of years. It is depicted on Egyptian tombs.

BASENJI

DOG ANATOMY

THE BASIC DESIGN of the dog is that of a highly developed carnivorous mammal of the hunt. Over the centuries, humans have modified dog anatomy to exploit particular talents, and for aesthetic appeal.

Insulating coat

Loin

Brush, or tail

Croup

Flank

Stifle

Lower thigh

Hock

Pastern

Knee

INTERNAL ANATOMY

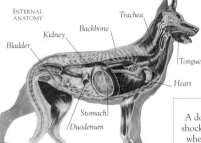

Trachea

Backbone

Kidney

Bladder

Tongue

Heart

Stomach

Duodenum

INTERNAL ORGANS

The organs of the dog are essentially the same as those of humans, and function in the same way. Although its attitude toward food is that of a hunter-scavenger, the dog is not a pure carnivore, tending toward an omnivorous diet. Its digestive system can cope with anything from fruit and nuts to shellfish and raw meat.

PAWS

A dog's paws carry pads that act as shock absorbers, provide a good grip when running, and contain sweat glands. The claws, unlike those of most cats, cannot be retracted.

Small pads not sensitive to hot and cold

Stopper pad prevents slipping after a jump

Large pad bears most weight

Dewclaw

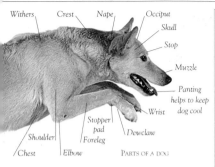

Withers Crest Nape Occiput
Skull
Stop
Muzzle

Panting
helps to keep
Wrist dog cool

Stopper
pad
Shoulder Foreleg Dewclaw
Chest Elbow PARTS OF A DOG

CLASSIC DESIGN

The classic canine design is seen in most wild
or feral dogs and many domesticated
mongrels: a lithe body, long legs, a long tail
for balance and communication, efficient
prick ears, and excellent vision – all ideal
features for a resourceful hunting animal
with plenty of stamina.

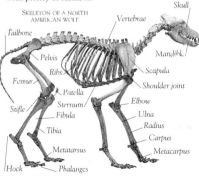

SKELETON OF A NORTH
AMERICAN WOLF
Vertebrae
Skull
Tailbone
Pelvis
Ribs
Scapula
Mandible
Femur
Shoulder joint
Patella
Stifle
Sternum
Elbow
Fibula
Ulna
Tibia
Radius
Carpus
Metatarsus
Metacarpus
Hock Phalanges

TEETH

An adult dog has 42
teeth. They include four
stabbing canine teeth
and four molar teeth called
carnassials that are
designed to shear through
tough flesh.

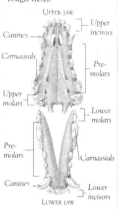

UPPER JAW

Canines — Upper
incisors

Carnassials

Upper — Pre-
molars — molars

Upper
molars — Lower
molars

Pre-
molars — Carnassials

Canines — Lower
incisors

LOWER JAW

THE SKELETON

The basic dog framework
provides strength, flexibility,
and speed. However, selective
breeding has resulted in some
breeds possessing weak areas.
Extra-long spines can lead to
"slipped disks"; compressed
skulls to breathing troubles; and
short legs to knee problems.

More on anatomy

All predatory animals depend on their sight, hearing, and sense of smell to catch prey. A dog's sense organs are some of the most sophisticated in the animal kingdom. Dogs' reproductive systems follow the basic mammalian pattern, but with some distinct features in the male.

Cerebral cortex

Frontal sinus

Nasal membranes

Vomeronasal organ

Tongue

Soft palate

Windpipe

CROSS SECTION OF THE HEAD

SMELL AND TASTE

Dogs are marvelous smellers, in fact about one million times better than humans. Their long noses contain "smelling membranes" about 40 times larger than ours. Taste is not as important, as dogs "gobble" rather than "savor" food.

SIGHT

Dogs' eyes are more sensitive to light and movement than ours and they can often "miss" creatures that stand very still. Yet shepherds claim their working dogs will react to hand signals at a distance of 0.6 miles (1 km). Dogs are not totally color-blind, but see mainly in black, white, and shades of gray. The anatomy of a dog's eye is very similar to ours.

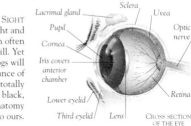

Lacrimal gland

Sclera

Uvea

Pupil

Optic nerve

Cornea

Iris covers anterior chamber

Retina

Lower eyelid

Third eyelid

Lens

CROSS SECTION OF THE EYE

DOG'S EYE VIEW 250°–290°

HUMAN'S EYE VIEW 210°

VISION

A dog has a wider field of vision than a human because its eyes are set toward the sides of its head. Its carnivorous, hunter ancestors needed lateral vision.

HEARING

Dogs have excellent hearing. Equipped with large external ears served by 17 muscles, they can prick and swivel these sound receivers to focus on the source of noise. They can register high-pitched sounds of 35,000 Hz (vibrations per second), compared to humans' 20,000 Hz. This greater hearing range assists in tracking down quarry.

Ear turns to detect sound

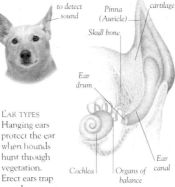

Ear cartilage

Pinna (Auricle)

Skull bone

Ear drum

Cochlea   *Organs of balance*   *Ear canal*

INSIDE THE EAR

EAR TYPES

Hanging ears protect the ear when hounds hunt through vegetation. Erect ears trap sound waves most effectively.

HANGING EARS   POINTED EARS

REPRODUCTIVE ORGANS

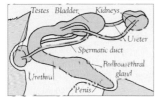

Testes Bladder Kidneys
Ureter
Spermatic duct
Bulbourethral gland
Urethra
Penis

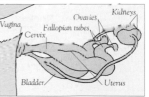

Ovaries Kidneys
Vagina Fallopian tubes
Cervix
Bladder Uterus

MALE

The dog's penis contains a bone, through which the urethra passes, and a bulbourethral gland that swells up, thereby "tying" the dog and bitch together during sexual intercourse.

FEMALE

The female has a typical mammalian arrangement: vagina, cervix, uterus, fallopian tubes, and ovaries. When a bitch is neutered, the ovaries, fallopian tubes, and uterus are removed surgically.

LIFE CYCLE OF DOGS

ON AVERAGE, a dog's life span is about 12 years, though small breeds generally live longer than larger ones. In terms of aging, the first year of a dog's life equals 15 human years, the second equals nine years, and thereafter each dog year counts for four human years.

GETTING ACQUAINTED

Exploratory sniffing before mating begins

THE "HEAT" PERIOD
The female is called the bitch. She becomes sexually mature at 8–12 months old. Twice a year, she goes into "heat," usually for 18–21 days. This is when ovulation occurs.

MATING

Female remains willing but passive

MATING
The male is sexually active all year and is attracted to the scent of a female in "heat." When a female is ready to mate, she draws her tail to one side. The transmission of sperm is completed within a minute but the couple remain "locked" together for half an hour.

DEVELOPMENT OF A PUPPY

7 DAYS
At this age the puppy only sleeps or nurses. Its eyes and ear canals are closed, but it responds to its mother's touch.

14 DAYS
The eyes are opening but they cannot focus properly for another 7 days. Between 13 and 17 days the puppy begins to hear.

3 WEEKS
At 3 weeks the puppy can focus its eyes and move around. Its nails should be trimmed to prevent it from scratching the mother.

---

1. The yolk sac provides nourishment to the embryo for the first few days

2. By the third week of pregnancy, the embryo has a developing head, eyes, and limbs

3. By midpregnancy, all the internal organs are developed

Yolk sac

Embryo

Most puppies will emerge head first in diving position

PREGNANCY

Pregnancy in the bitch lasts an average of 63 days. The swelling of her tummy is noticeable from the fifth week onward. The breasts and nipples become bigger, and milk can often be produced 5–6 days before labor begins.

4. At six weeks, the skeleton has developed

BIRTH

When the puppies are almost ready to be born, the mother may stop eating and find a nest site. She gives birth to the first puppy soon afterward, and may rest for minutes or hours after each puppy is born. Each puppy's placenta usually comes out within 15 minutes.

Mother sits contentedly while puppies nurse

Puppies huddle together for food and security

BONDING WITH MOTHER

30 DAYS
The puppy begins to play. Teething starts at 3–5 weeks. It should receive its first worming dosage.

6 WEEKS
Milk teeth are present, but the puppy is still nursing, and it should not be separated from its mother.

8 WEEKS
Mother and pup can be separated now, and the puppy should receive vaccinations against major diseases.

DOG BEHAVIOR

DOGS EXHIBIT A BROAD RANGE of behavior patterns that spring from their origins as social, hunting animals. Ear and tail movements are obviously expressive, but all patterns are vital rituals that express a dog's relationship with its environment.

SCENT GLANDS
Distinctive scents are produced by sebaceous glands in the dog's anal sacs (anal glands) that are passed on to feces, and by sweat glands in the hind paws. These scents lay down sniffable information that only dogs can interpret.

SCENT MARKING
A dog marks out territory via deposits of urine or feces, or by scratching the ground with its hind legs.

Dog shows interest in a scent

HOWLING
Howling is an ancient form of dog communication. Wild dogs and wolves howl to let other pack members know where they are and, in some cases, to inform strangers that they are in possession of territory. It can also be a sign of distress or loneliness.

DIGGING
Dogs inherit their love of digging from their ancestors, who stored food in order to survive when hunting was poor. It leads well-fed dogs to bury bones and dig them up later.

AGGRESSION

Aggression can indicate possessiveness of prized objects, territory, or animals. It can be directed at outsiders who are not members of the home pack. Fear and pain also cause aggression.

DOMINANCE

Dogs asserting their dominance make eye contact, with tail raised and ears erect, and often place their neck on the other dog's shoulder. Size, though helpful, does not necessarily affect dominance.

Tail carried high indicates boldness

SUBMISSION

Submissive individuals in the canine hierarchy reveal their position by their crouched postures, and by rolling onto their backs, looking away, and appearing meek and defenseless.

PLAY BOW

The play bow, often exhibited by puppies, is a clear request to human or fellow dog to meet on friendly terms. Indicating total lack of aggressive intent, it is usually an invitation to play.

Body is lowered to ground

Human pack leader offers food

Dog pack leader shows authority by rising above other dogs

HIERARCHY

Packs of wild canines have leaders to exercise authority and coordinate activity. This is usually, but not always, a male. Gatherings of domestic dogs behave in the same way.

INTRODUCTION TO BREEDS

AMONG DOMESTICATED ANIMALS only the dog has been selectively bred to produce such a wide variety of types. Worldwide, there are over 500 different breeds. National kennel clubs differ in the way they group breeds so, for the purposes of this book, general categories have been used.

CHOW CHOW

GUNDOGS

Gundogs were developed to pick up the air scents of game and also be good sporting companions. They are highly responsive and amenable workers. Field trials are held regularly to test working skills.

IRISH RED AND WHITE SETTER

SPECIAL DOGS

This is a miscellaneous collection of breeds. Many, such as the Chow Chow, are highly distinctive, and some have specialized in particular types of work. Most make good companions; many popular pets fall into this category.

HERDING DOGS AND GUARD DOGS

These dogs were bred to protect and herd livestock, work as guards, pull and carry loads, or assist police and armed forces. Most of these dogs are happiest when they have access to open spaces and a job to do.

BORDER COLLIES HERDING SHEEP

HOUNDS

These athletes with sensitive noses and sharp eyes were the first dogs used by humans. They helped their (much slower) masters by hunting down animals, such as deer, for food.

FOXHOUNDS

TERRIERS

Developed from hounds to tackle small, burrowing animals, terriers are generally small, short-legged, stocky animals with alert and spirited temperaments. No group of dogs is more expert at burrowing than terriers.

NORFOLK TERRIERS

TOY DOGS

These breeds' main function is to be loyal, decorative, and friendly companions. Many are useful for raising the alarm and nipping intruders' ankles. Small and dainty, they play a vital role in people's lives.

PEKINGESE

MONGRELS

Most dogs in the world are mongrels or "crossbreed" dogs that have interbred at random. Apart from their individual endearing qualities, they are often better-tempered, less disease-prone, and more adaptable than purebreds.

HOUNDS AND GUNDOGS

BIG GAME HUNTERS

SINCE ANCIENT TIMES some dog breeds have been
developed to tackle the largest or fiercest kinds
of animal quarry, such as deer, wolves, and even large
cats. Sometimes the subject of legend, these big-game
hunters are statuesque, fast, and fearless.

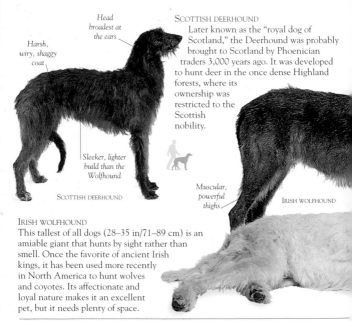

Head broadest at the ears

Harsh, wiry, shaggy coat

Sleeker, lighter build than the Wolfhound

SCOTTISH DEERHOUND

SCOTTISH DEERHOUND

Later known as the "royal dog of
Scotland," the Deerhound was probably
brought to Scotland by Phoenician
traders 3,000 years ago. It was developed
to hunt deer in the once dense Highland
forests, where its
ownership was
restricted to the
Scottish
nobility.

Muscular, powerful thighs

IRISH WOLFHOUND

IRISH WOLFHOUND

This tallest of all dogs (28–35 in/71–89 cm) is an
amiable giant that hunts by sight rather than
smell. Once the favorite of ancient Irish
kings, it has been used more recently
in North America to hunt wolves
and coyotes. Its affectionate and
loyal nature makes it an excellent
pet, but it needs plenty of space.

RHODESIAN RIDGEBACK
Also known as the Rhodesian Lion Dog, this tough but quiet-tempered breed was developed in South Africa by crossing European mastiffs, terriers, and bloodhounds with local African dogs. Hunting in packs, it has tracked not only lion, but leopard, buffalo, and large antelope.

Broad, flat skull

RHODESIAN RIDGEBACK

Coat is sleek and glossy

Ridge of hair grows in opposite direction to rest of coat

Long, powerful back

Long, slightly pointed muzzle

AMERICAN STAGHOUND
The rugged Staghound is a descendant of the Deerhound and Irish Wolfhound. In the 1800s it was exported to the US, where it was used to clear the land of wolves and coyotes. After settlements were established, hunting continued as a sport. Today it hunts deer; it is also becoming a popular companion.

Eyes bright and alert

Long, powerful jaw

Strong, straight legs

AMERICAN STAGHOUND

Rough, hardy coat

LONG-LEGGED ATHLETES

SPEED AND AGILITY characterize the
Sloughi, Afghan, Borzoi, and Saluki.
With long legs, supple backs, and
sharp vision, they hunt by sight,
usually in open desert or savanna.
All originated in southwest Asia.

*Fawn coat
provides
camouflage
in desert*

SLOUGHI
Bedouin used the Sloughi to
pursue gazelle and hare in
the Arabian desert, and
probably brought it to North
Africa over 1,000 years
ago. Although loyal to its
owner, this high-strung and
sensitive breed can be
aloof with strangers.

Deep chest

*Oval and
narrow feet,
with strong,
thick pads*

SLOUGHI

*Hair becomes
short and close
on back*

AFGHAN HOUND

*Long, silky
hair*

*Muzzle is long
and elegant*

AFGHAN HOUND
An ancient text
from Egypt, written in
3500 B.C., first described the
Afghan or "monkey-faced"
hound. How the breed traveled
from the Middle East to
Afghanistan, where the
insulating coat was
developed, is not known.
It is still used to guard
sheep and goats.

BORZOI

The origins of the Borzoi go back to medieval Russia. First bred to protect its masters from local wolves, by the 16th century the Borzoi was a distinct breed used by the Tsars for wolf hunting. Outside Russia, the Borzoi has been bred as an amiable companion.

Powerful jaws

BORZOI

Long, silky, white hair with darker markings

Long, feathered tail

Long, mobile ears hang close to face

Long, muscular neck

SALUKI

Deep chest built for stamina

HUNTING IN INDIA

SALUKI

Akbar, Mogul emperor of India (1542–1605), is shown pursuing blackbuck with Saluki-type hounds (above). This ancient, elegant breed was carried to the hunt on camels to protect its feet from the burning desert sand.

31

ON THE SCENT

ALL DOGS, but particularly breeds
with long muzzles and those
developed for scent-tracking,
are much better "sniffers" than
humans. Hounds that rely on
sight hunt silently, while scent
hounds howl or bark when
they find a trail.

*Thin, soft ears
tend to curl
inward and
backward*

BLOODHOUND

Deep-set eyes

BLOODHOUND
This ancient dog, the
legendary workmate of
famous detectives, has
outstanding scenting
ability. It originated in Belgium
over 1,000 years ago, from hounds
bred by Benedictine monks at
the abbey of St. Hubert.

*Characteristic
dewlap*

BASSET HOUND
The Basset arose in 16th-
century France from short-
legged, "dwarf" mutations
of bloodhounds. At one
time the Basset made a
skilled hunter of rabbit
and hare; today this
characterful breed is very
popular as a pet.

*Slightly
sunken eyes*

*Long ears
extending
down face*

*Large
feet*

*Elbows are
set against
the chest*

BASSET HOUND

Powerful, muscular body

Black nose with very open nostrils

PORCELAINE

Long, slender neck

Fine-textured, very short hair with a high sheen

PORCELAINE

This good-looking French dog has a translucent coat that gleams like porcelain. It was developed in the 17th century as a packhunter of game, but almost disappeared during the French Revolution. Luckily, it was saved by Swiss breeders who introduced Swiss hound blood into the breed.

Strong, well-knuckled feet

Low-set, pendulous ears

SEGUGIO ITALIANO

Resembling the coursing hounds of the Egyptian pharaohs, the Segugio has inherited the long legs of a sight hound and the head of a scent hound. Its uncanny sense of smell makes it a valued hunting dog in Italy.

Coat is dense, short and glossy

SEGUGIO ITALIANO

Delicate, sickle-shaped tail

Feet are oval, like those of a hare

"SNIFFER" FACTS

- A human nose has 5 million sensory ("sniffing") cells, while the average dog has more than 200 million.
- The Bloodhound has been known to follow a trail that is more than 14 days old.

After fox, rabbit, and hare

Scent hounds such as the Foxhound and Beagle are in their element when on the trail of fox or hare, in tandem with other noisy pack members. These perky dogs are good natured, loyal, and have great stamina, but they can be willful!

BEAGLE

Muscular hind legs

Pendulous ears

BEAGLE
The cheerful, sprightly Beagle is a fine rabbit hunter who also makes a superb companion. Its origins lie in medieval French hare hounds called "begles," the Kerry Beagle (a small bloodhound-type dog), and the Southern English Hound.

FOXHOUNDS GATHERING FOR THE HUNT

ENGLISH FOXHOUND
Strong and intelligent, the English Foxhound was developed in the 15th century. At one time, the shape and size of individuals varied across Britain. Today the breed is standardized.

AMERICAN FOXHOUND
The American Foxhound inherited blood from the English and French Foxhound and the Kerry Beagle, but has longer legs and lighter bones.

Coonhounds

These North American dogs are specialists who not only trail racoon, opossum, and squirrel, they "tree" their quarry. Once they have cornered their quarry in a tree they sit beneath it, baying distinctively until the hunters arrive.

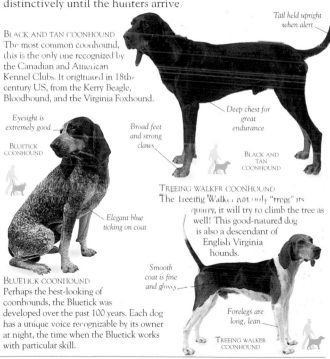

Tail held upright when alert

BLACK AND TAN COONHOUND
The most common coonhound, this is the only one recognized by the Canadian and American Kennel Clubs. It originated in 18th-century US, from the Kerry Beagle, Bloodhound, and the Virginia Foxhound.

Eyesight is extremely good

BLUETICK COONHOUND

Broad feet and strong claws

Deep chest for great endurance

BLACK AND TAN COONHOUND

TREEING WALKER COONHOUND
The Treeing Walker not only "trees" its quarry, it will try to climb the tree as well! This good-natured dog is also a descendant of English Virginia hounds.

Elegant blue ticking on coat

Smooth coat is fine and glossy

BLUETICK COONHOUND
Perhaps the best-looking of coonhounds, the Bluetick was developed over the past 100 years. Each dog has a unique voice recognizable by its owner at night, the time when the Bluetick works with particular skill.

Forelegs are long, lean

TREEING WALKER COONHOUND

DACHSHUNDS

THE DACHSHUND, whose German name means "badger dog," is much more like a terrier than a hound in size and function. In the 15th century, the first dachshunds, which were much larger than their modern descendants, tackled badgers and foxes underground – a formidable task calling for strength and great courage.

A ROYAL PET
Queen Victoria of Britain was a great dog lover. This 19th-century photograph pictures her with a favorite dachshund, named Dackel.

Narrow forehead is slightly arched

Long, thin, tapering muzzle

SMOOTH-HAIRED DACHSHUND

SMOOTH-HAIRED DACHSHUND
Although ancient representations of long-bodied, little-legged dogs have been found in Egypt, Greece, China, and South America, many believe the dachshund is a true German development. The Smooth- or Short-Haired dog is probably the oldest type.

Strong, prominent eyebrows

Distinctive beard

WIRE-HAIRED MINIATURE DACHSHUND

WIRE-HAIRED MINIATURE DACHSHUND
Smooth-Haired, Wire-Haired, and Long-Haired
Dachshunds all come in standard and miniature sizes.
The Wire-Haired type was created by
crossing Smooth-Haired Dachshunds with
rough-haired Pinschers.

Long neck

Miniatures are small enough to follow rabbits down holes

Normal-sized skull

Long spine

Very short, "dwarfed" leg bones and normal-sized feet

SKELETON

DWARFED SKELETON
Selective breeding has dwarfed
the dachshund's skeleton. As
a result, it is structurally weak;
the long, unsupported spine
renders the dog prone to
"slipped-disc" problems.

LONG-HAIRED MINIATURE DACHSHUND

Coat longest on neck and underparts

LONG-HAIRED DACHSHUND
This type of dachshund was
developed by crossing the
Smooth-Haired Dachshund
with short-legged spaniels.
The Long-Haired
Dachshund certainly has an
outgoing, affectionate nature
similar to that of spaniels and,
like all other dachshunds, is lively
and determined.

3 7

SPRINTERS

HERE ARE THE OLYMPIC 100-meter stars of the canine world. Possessing lithe, slim bodies, long legs, and sleek coats, these aerodynamic animals were specially bred over the centuries for hunting agile, swift game, and for sport.

Powerful hindquarters

Legs are sinewy and well-boned

Very deep chest aids breathing

RACING
The highest speed achieved by a racing greyhound, Star Title, was 41.83 mph (67.36 km/h) at Wyong, NSW, Australia in 1994.

GREYHOUND RACE

GREYHOUND
This fastest of all dogs originated in the Middle East, arriving in Europe with early Phoenician trading ships during the first millennium B.C. Its name derives from the old Saxon word *grei*, meaning fine, or beautiful. Found on the coat of arms of Charles V of France and Henry VIII of England, it is the most common heraldic dog, signifying elegant athleticism and loyalty.

Flexible spine for running rapidly

LURCHER RUNNING

IBIZAN HOUND

This elegant dog originated in the Balearic Islands, spread to mainland Spain and then France, where it was called the Charnique. A fine courser and retriever, it is also a loyal and affectionate companion.

Ears erect when alert

IBIZAN HOUND

Short, sleek coat

Muscular legs

CIRNECO DELL'ETNA

Rarely seen outside Italy, this true Sicilian has remained a pure breed for 2,000 years because of its isolation on the island. A hunter by sight and scent, it is an outdoor type and not an easy pet.

Large ears funnel sounds to assist in hunting

Long, straight muzzle

CIRNECO DELL'ETNA

ITALIAN GREYHOUND

The most delicate of dogs, this amazing sprinter can catch a hare, but is mainly valued as a perfect companion around. It was created in Classical Greece and ancient Egypt, from small greyhounds.

Ears well back on head

Straight, fine-boned legs

ITALIAN GREYHOUND

LURCHER

This dog was first bred by gypsies in Great Britain and Ireland from greyhounds and terriers; its name comes from the Romany word "lur," meaning thief. A favorite of poachers and rabbit and hare coursers, the Lurcher is not a recognized breed.

WHIPPETS

Nicknamed "the poor man's racehorse" (easy and inexpensive to keep), the Whippet was popular as a racing dog among working men in 19th-century northern England. It contains the blood of greyhounds and terriers.

OTHER HOUNDS

THERE ARE SOME HOUND BREEDS that the ordinary dog lover rarely sees. These dogs are either localized to a particular country or region or, for various reasons, have become less popular as working animals.

Profuse hair covers face

OTTERHOUND

The cheerful, courageous Otterhound originated in Britain almost 1,000 years ago. With its bristly topcoat and woolly overcoat for protection, it plunged enthusiastically into freezing cold rivers on the trail of otters. Now that otter hunting is banned in Britain, this hound is rarely seen. However, it makes an excellent companion.

Skull is domed, elongated and not too wide

Ears hang to tip of nose when scenting

GRAND

PETIT

OTTERHOUND

Coat has slightly oily texture

BASSET GRIFFON VENDÉEN

Long popular in France, this breed comes in two sizes, the Grand and the Petit. It was developed from ancient Gallic hunting hounds. By the 19th century the breed was, in essence, a rough-coated (griffon) form of the Basset Hound. Both sizes are energetic and affectionate.

Short legs

BILLY

Rare even in its native France, the Billy is a scent hound developed in the 19th century for tracking deer and wild boar. It is named after the Château de Billy, whose owner crossed the now-extinct Céris, Montaimboeuf, and Larrye breeds. Only two Billys survived World War II!

Long ears are set below eye level

Tail is long and strong

Thighs are only moderately muscled

BILLY

Short, smooth coat with brown ticking

Neck is strong and muscular

Forelegs strong without being stocky

Clearly defined colored markings

SABUESO ESPANOL

SABUESO ESPAÑOL

Much of the ancestry of the Sabueso or Spanish Hound is shared with the Bloodhound, and the blood of the old, now-extinct, white Talbot Hound. A tough, tireless tracker of game, it can be temperamental and difficult as a companion animal.

ST. HUBERT JURA HOUND

Long, lean head has well-defined stop

Deep rib cage

ST. HUBERT JURA HOUND

Powerful and deceptively fast and agile, this Swiss hound accompanies hunters who go out on foot in search of small alpine game. An avid tracker, it bays loudly when following a scent. The St. Hubert Jura is a loyal and affectionate companion animal, but it is sometimes headstrong, needing firm handling.

RETRIEVERS

RETRIEVERS WERE DEVELOPED from the water-loving Newfoundland to collect "downed" game. Apart from being efficient working dogs, retrievers comprise some of the most valuable service and companion animals in the canine world.

LABRADOR RETRIEVER

Medium-length jaws are used deftly when working

LABRADOR RETRIEVER
This most popular retriever originated in 19th-century Newfoundland, where it was used to haul fishermen's nets ashore. Today, apart from being a gundog, Labradors act as guide dogs and have also been trained to detect explosives.

Broad head has pronounced stop (dip)

GOLDEN RETRIEVER

Coat is short and silky

Feet are round and compact

GOLDEN RETRIEVER
Originally a wildfowl hunter, this dog may be a descendant of a mysterious Russian dog, or of other retrievers and the Tweed Water Spaniel. Like the Labrador, its gentle nature makes it an ideal pet.

RETRIEVING IN WATER

FLAT-COATED RETRIEVER

Bred from the Labrador and Newfoundland, this gundog was a gamekeeper's favorite at the turn of the century. After World War II, it was almost extinct, but its numbers are now increasing.

Gentle stop delineates skull from muzzle

Shiny, short coat with waterproof undercoat

FLAT-COATED RETRIEVER

Wedge-shaped head with fairly small ears

Powerful, compact, well-muscled body

NOVA SCOTIA DUCK TOLLING RETRIEVER

In old English, the word "toilen" meant to entice; this rather oddly named Canadian breed does specialize in enticing. It lures curious ducks within range of the concealed hunters' guns by creating a disturbance at the water's edge.

CURLY-COATED RETRIEVER

The rarest and oldest of all the British retrievers, this breed was once immensely popular as a water retriever. Like other water dogs, its coat is waterproof, being composed of small, tight curls.

Head sits comfortably on long neck

Crisp curls over entire body

Deep chest is broad

CURLY-COATED RETRIEVER

CHESAPEAKE BAY RETRIEVER

Wide-set eyes are inquiring

Wavy coat occurs in various shades of red or orange

CHESAPEAKE BAY RETRIEVER

This American retriever was first used for retrieving waterfowl in the cold waters of the Chesapeake Bay. A tough and resolute working dog, it sports a coarse, oily, quick-drying coat. Like all retrievers, it makes a delightful companion.

POINTERS

FOR CENTURIES, certain
hunting dogs have been
used to "point" out game
by adopting a distinctive stance when
they have located their quarry. Their head
is extended toward the target, tail and one
foreleg raised expectantly. The first
pointers assisted their masters in netting
birds, such as quail and partridge.

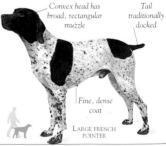

Oval, well-arched toes

*Well-defined
stop on the
muzzle*

*Ticking
present
on this
specimen*

*Medium-length ears,
lying close
to head*

ENGLISH POINTER

ENGLISH POINTER
The Pointer, or English Pointer, arose from
the introduction to England, in the early
18th century, of the Spanish Pointer
(a rather cumbersome dog which kept its
nose to the ground). The integration of
Greyhound and English Foxhound blood
increased the speed and air-scenting talents
of the breed.

*Convex head has
broad, rectangular
muzzle*

*Tail
traditionally
docked*

*Fine, dense
coat*

LARGE FRENCH POINTER
One of France's oldest breeds, the Large
French Pointer is an imposing dog, with a
strong, well-muscled physique. It
originated during the 1600s in the
Pyrenean region of France and is
descended from the old, extinct Southern
Hound. It is also a close relative of the
Italian and Spanish Pointers.

LARGE FRENCH
POINTER

ENGLISH POINTER

Tail is level with back, and lashes from side to side when dog is in motion

GERMAN WIREHAIRED POINTER
First recognized in Germany in 1870, this pointer is an all-around dog that flushes game, points and retrieves in water or on land, and can be trained to hunt game bird, rabbit, fox, deer, or boar. It is the product of the selective breeding of Broken-Coated and Short-Haired pointers, Pudelpointers, and French griffons.

Pronounced beard

Harsh, wiry overcoat

Straight forelegs

Powerful hind legs

GERMAN WIREHAIRED POINTER

Docked tail

Short coat may have patches of colour

SPANISH POINTER

Large head

Wrinkled dewlap

Hanging ears

SPANISH POINTER
The Spanish Pointer is the most ancient of all pointer breeds, one of the oldest gundog types still around, and the basis of most modern hunting dogs that point game. It arose in the 15th century, probably from crosses between extinct pointers such as the Perdiguero Navarro and other lighter-built pointers.

More pointers

Beginning in the 16th century, when Spanish hunting techniques were in fashion, the development of pointing dogs spread throughout Europe and the Americas. Dogs specialized for different kinds of hunting and for particular types of terrain were gradually evolved through selective breeding.

ABOUT TO "POINT"

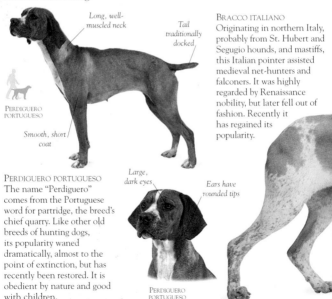

Long, well-muscled neck

Tail traditionally docked

PERDIGUERO PORTUGUESO

Smooth, short coat

BRACCO ITALIANO
Originating in northern Italy, probably from St. Hubert and Segugio hounds, and mastiffs, this Italian pointer assisted medieval net-hunters and falconers. It was highly regarded by Renaissance nobility, but later fell out of fashion. Recently it has regained its popularity.

PERDIGUERO PORTUGUESO
The name "Perdiguero" comes from the Portuguese word for partridge, the breed's chief quarry. Like other old breeds of hunting dogs, its popularity waned dramatically, almost to the point of extinction, but has recently been restored. It is obedient by nature and good with children.

Large, dark eyes

Ears have rounded tips

PERDIGUERO PORTUGUESO

BRAQUE DU BOURBONNAIS

The Bourbonnais Pointer is the oldest and most even-tempered of the French pointers. It was first described in 1598 in Bourbon, a former province of central France. A multipurpose hunting dog, it flourished in France during the 1800s but then declined in numbers after World War I, only to be rediscovered recently.

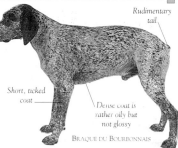

Rudimentary tail

Short, ticked coat

Dense coat is rather oily but not glossy

BRAQUE DU BOURBONNAIS

BRACCO ITALIANO

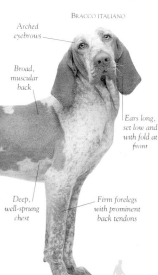

Arched eyebrows

Broad, muscular back

Ears long, set low and with fold at front

Deep, well-sprung chest

Firm forelegs with prominent back tendons

PUDELPOINTER

This rare German pointer possesses excellent qualities as an all-around, all-weather gundog, but has never been very popular. It was created in the 19th century by Baron von Zedlitz, who selectively crossbred seven poodles and almost 100 pointers.

Large, black nose has wide nostrils

Coat is short, rough, and waterproof

SETTERS

WHEREAS THE POINTER locates its quarry and "points," the setter, after pinpointing the game, crouches down or "sets," head pointed toward the target. A well-trained setter will remain in this position, utterly immobile, for an hour or so if necessary, awaiting the hunter's next command.

Long, velvety ears

ENGLISH SETTER

Long, muscular legs

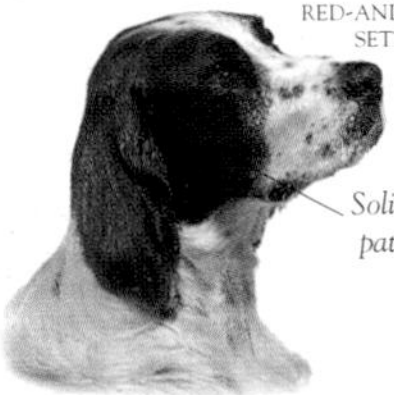

IRISH RED-AND-WHITE SETTER

Solid red patches

IRISH SETTER

Rich, chestnut coat

IRISH SETTER
The Irish or Red Setter, which, like all setters, is descended from early Spanish spaniels and pointers, was originally a red or white dog with shorter legs than the modern type. The gleaming, chestnut-red color was achieved in the 19th century. It has a boisterous, friendly character, and can be high-strung and disobedient if not handled firmly.

Luxurious feathering

ENGLISH SETTER

The English Setter is an elegant, silky-coated, well-mannered dog needing lots of exercise. It makes a fine children's pet. Two strains of the breed were developed in the 19th century, the Laverack and the Llewellyn.

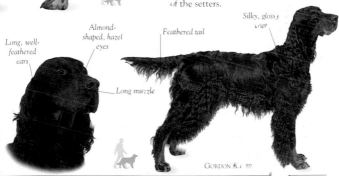

Feathered tail tapers to fine point

Wavy topcoat with fleecy undercoat

THE FIRST OF SEPTEMBER BY
JAMES HARDY JR, (1832-89)

GORDON SETTER

This handsome dog was first seen in 18th-century Scotland. The 4th Duke of Richmond and Gordon selectively bred Scottish black and tan setters, which had existed since at least the 1600s. It may also have some Bloodhound and collie blood. A loyal and obedient companion, it is the strongest, heaviest, and slowest of the setters.

Long, well-feathered ears

Almond-shaped, hazel eyes

Long muzzle

Feathered tail

Silky, glossy coat

GORDON SETTER

SPANIELS

SPANIELS MAKE UP THE LARGEST subdivision of gundogs, and include some of the oldest dog breeds in the world. All originated from Spanish stock; the word "spaniel" is derived from "Espaignol," the Old French word for "Spanish."

Skull and muzzle of equal length

Flat-lying coat of silky hair

ENGLISH COCKER

ENGLISH COCKER SPANIEL
The word "cocker" is short for "woodcocker." It refers to the dog's aptitude for flushing woodcock. In the field it works tirelessly with skill and enthusiasm, although it is most popular nowadays as a loyal pet.

Domed head shape

Clearly defined stop

AMERICAN COCKER SPANIEL

Lobular ears

Profuse covering of wavy or flat, silky hair

AMERICAN COCKER SPANIEL
This beautiful and playful breed also works well and makes a perfect companion. It is the smallest of the spaniels, with shorter legs, back, and muzzle than the English Cocker. The key dog in the history of the breed was a mutant, Red Brucie, who, in the 1920s, began the modern American Cocker line.

Rounded, firm feet with thick pads

Well-feathered tail

Ears shaped like vine leaves

Short legs and large feet

CLUMBER SPANIEL
It is believed that this rather heavyset spaniel evolved in France, perhaps possessing some Basset Hound and Bloodhound blood. It is renowned for its stealth and silence when working in the field.

Large, square skull

CLUMBER SPANIEL

Heavy brow with wrinkled eyelids

SPANIEL WITH GAME
Spaniels specialize in flushing (disturbing birds into flight toward hunters). They then retrieve the fallen game in their soft mouths without damaging it further.

Quarry is retrieved without further harm

Strong jaw

Lobe-shaped ears

Patches of brown or black

ENGLISH SPRINGER SPANIEL
The English Springer Spaniel is considered among the finest of gundogs and a delightful pet. It became a distinct breed in the late 19th century. Strong, fast, and with great stamina, the "Springing Spaniel" will work in all conditions – it will even retrieve in icy water.

Long legs

ENGLISH SPRINGER SPANIEL

Out in the field

When a spaniel smells game, it rushes in to flush it, making it fly or run. Once the hunter shoots, the spaniel waits for a command, finds the game, and then brings it back to the hunter.

SHOOTING 18TH-CENTURY STYLE

GERMAN SPANIEL
Although this first-class working spaniel is called a "Wachtelhund" ("quail dog") in German, it is actually a talented all-purpose dog with an acute sense of smell. Seldom seen outside Germany, the breed was developed at the end of the 19th century.

Hanging ears covered with long hair

Low-set ears hang with graceful folds

FIELD SPANIEL

Very long rib cage

Weather-resistant, glossy coat

Feathering present on backs of forelegs

GERMAN SPANIEL

FIELD SPANIEL
Once considered a variety of the English Cocker Spaniel, the Field Spaniel was recognized as a distinct breed in 1892. Subsequent breeding, aimed purely at the show ring, led to a dramatic loss of ability in the field. By the end of World War II, it was almost extinct. Fortunately, the introduction of fresh English Cocker and Springer Spaniel blood in the 1960s revived the breed.

DUTCH PARTRIDGE SPANIEL

Broad, powerful back is longer than the dog is high

Forelegs are straight and muscular

Medium length coat is long on neck and chest

DUTCH PARTRIDGE SPANIEL

This ancient breed is descended from dogs used by Dutch net-hunters who worked the fens of the Drente province in the Middle Ages. A kindly, multi-purpose dog that seems half-spaniel, half-setter, it does not look very different from its forebears of four centuries ago.

Rather short ears with pointed tips

BRITTANY

Body hair is fine and dense with sparse feathering

BRITTANY

The Brittany, a superb working dog and the most popular native breed in France, is the only spaniel that points its game well. Bred to retrieve waterfowl in the 1700s, it has also become a favorite of American hunters and is a popular and affectionate companion.

Flat, relatively long, straight coat

BLUE PICARDY SPANIEL

Ram-shaped muzzle with prominent nose

BLUE PICARDY SPANIEL

Developed in northeastern France in the 1700s from crosses between English Setters and Picardy Spaniels, this energetic, hardworking, and good-natured breed has a shining black coat ticked with white to produce a blue effect. It was first used to retrieve snipe from the Picardy marshes.

WATER DOGS

MANY DOGS, particularly the bigger, sporting, outdoor types, love to play around in the water. But some, through selective breeding, have become specialized workers in watery places and wet weather.

Plume of hair permits tail to float

PORTUGUESE WATER DOG
This ancient fisherman's dog once retrieved lost tackle and nets and swam, carrying messages or small loads, from boat to boat. Its coat was cut poodle-fashion – short on the hind parts to reduce drag while swimming, long on the chest as a protection against cold water, and with a tuft of hair on the tail to help it float.

Hair clipped for work and for showing

PORTUGUESE WATER DOG

Face is fully covered with hair

BARBET

Woolly coat curls slightly

BARBET
This ancient French hunting breed once retrieved fallen arrows and game birds from water. Its dense coat is watertight and the large feet have broad webbing between the toes. Its need of intensive coat care has prevented it from becoming a popular pet.

SPANISH WATER DOG

Related to the Portuguese Water Dog and perhaps carrying poodle genes, this dog is rarely seen outside Spain. Once it was principally a fisherman's dog, but nowadays most are found in southern Spain herding goats or retrieving ducks for hunters. The nonshedding, heavily corded coat insulates it well against cold water.

Hair bleaches in sunshine

SPANISH WATER DOG

Nonshedding coat forms heavy cords of hair

IRISH WATER SPANIEL

Curly topknot of hair hangs just above eyes

Long neck carries head well above body

IRISH WATER SPANIEL

Nicknamed "the clown of the spaniel family" because of its lively behavior, this is a descendant of old Portuguese water dogs brought by visiting fishermen to Ireland in the 19th century. Introduced into the US long before the founding of the American Kennel Club in 1884, it was America's most popular retriever for many years.

Each cord of hair has to be groomed separately

Slightly rusty color is not uncommon

HUNGARIAN PULI

HUNGARIAN PULI

The long, heavily corded coat of the Puli is almost waterproof and demands the regular grooming of each separate cord of hair. Probably a descendant of the ancient Tibetan Dog and an ancestor of the poodle, this dog was once used for herding and, more recently, for retrieving and companionship.

OTHER GUNDOGS

AS THE BOW, SPEAR, AND NET of the hunter were superseded by the gun, many more breeds of multipurpose dogs came into being to assist hunters employing the new firearm techniques.

Rather light tail

WEIMARANER

Aristocratic head with long muzzle and skull

High-set ears are slightly folded

Coat is sleek, smooth, and short

ITALIAN SPINONE
This cheerful, even-tempered dog originated in northern Italy and can be traced back to the 13th century. Still used as a gundog and in field trials, it also makes an easy-going and obedient companion animal.

WEIMARANER
Courageous and willful, this dog was once used to hunt wolves, bears, and wild boar. Later it was more commonly employed to track and retrieve game birds. Originating in 17th-century Germany, its breeding was not permitted outside that country until the 1930s.

Long-haired coat is most prominent on ears

Thick coat is slightly wiry

ITALIAN SPINONE

Long hair on mustache and beard

LONG-HAIRED WEIMARANER

WIREHAIRED VIZSLA
Crossbreeding between the German Wirehaired Pointer and the Hungarian Vizsla, during the 1930s gave rise to this loyal, obedient, but rare breed.

Gentle and alert eyes are darker than coat

Wiry beard on muzzle

Long, elegant neck

WIREHAIRED VIZSLA

GUNDOG FACTS

• In the 17th century, hunters believed that rubbing vinegar onto gundogs' noses would improve their scenting ability.

• The first registration of the American Kennel Club was of Adonis, an English Setter, in 1878.

HUNGARIAN VIZSLA
This gentle hunting dog is an outdoor type that hates confinement and urban life. Some claim its forebears arrived in the 11th century when the Magyar hordes invaded Hungary. Others believe it is a cross between the now-extinct Pannonian Hound and the Yellow Turkish Dog.

HUNGARIAN VIZSLA

Hair is short, dense, and shiny

CZESKY FOUSEK

Soft, dense undercoat and rough topcoat

Muzzle is slightly longer than skull

CZESKY FOUSEK
A classic Bohemian breed, this dog makes a popular, all-around hunter, equally at home on land or in water, as well as a loving pet, particularly for children. Although its ancestors were pointing and setting wildfowl in the 15th century, the Czesky Fousek was established as a breed in Czechoslovakia only about 100 years ago.

Well-muscled elbows on straight, lean legs

HERDING AND GUARD DOGS

THE VERSATILE SHEPHERD

SOME OF THE MOST industrious and responsible working dogs are those bred originally to handle livestock. The German Shepherd Dog, particularly, displays abilities and versatility that are highly valued in other important types of work.

Erect, alert ears

GERMAN SHEPHERD DOG
The world's most numerous dog has its origins in herding dogs bred by Max von Stephanitz in the late 1800s. The result was a responsive breed used by police, the armed services, and blind people.

Relatively long body

Powerful thighs

GERMAN SHEPHERD DOG

Rounded feet with short nails

Back is broad, strong, and solid

Both upper and lower thighs are well-muscled

SHILOH SHEPHERD
In the 1980s an American breeder developed the Shiloh Shepherd by careful selective breeding of German Shepherds, to avoid any tendency toward nervousness or congenital bone disease. With breeders emphasizing quality of temperament, the Shiloh makes an agreeable pet.

Thick coat on chest

SHILOH SHEPHERD

POLICE DOG
Shepherds are trained by police to guard premises or personnel, apprehend criminals, sniff out explosives or drugs, and search for victims buried under rubble.

POLICE DOG AND HANDLER

LAEKENOIS
Closely related to the German Shepherd are Belgian Shepherd Dogs. Some countries classify four Belgian types: the Groenendael, the Malinois, the Tervuren, and the Laekenois – the rarest.

LAEKENOIS

Fawn colored coat

Long, smooth black hair

BELGIAN SHEPHERD

BELGIAN SHEPHERD
The Belgian Shepherd, highly robust and in need of early training, is called the Groenendael in Europe. In the US, the Malinois and Tervuren are recognized separately, and the Laekenois not at all.

TERVUREN
Very similar to the Groenendael and sharing the same ancestry, this superb Belgian livestock herder is in demand as a skillful police dog, particularly as a scent detector.

Feathered coat

TERVUREN

IMPROVING DOG STOCKS

SAARLOOS WOLFHOUND
In 1921, Dutchman Leendert Saarloos began an experiment to improve the qualities of the German Shepherd by introducing wolf blood. The result was the Saarloos Wolfhound, recognized as a new breed in 1975.

GUARDIANS OF THE FLOCK

SOME OF THESE livestock working breeds are
more commonly seen in the role of family
pets, but there are those, such the
Australian Cattle Dog, that are still
very important farmers' assistants in
their native lands.

*Hair extends
over eyes*

OLD ENGLISH SHEEPDOG
This amiable character
is one of England's oldest
breeds of sheepdog,
developed as a herder of
cattle and sheep in the
19th century. Its
forebears may include
the Bearded Collie and
the Briard. With its
rolling gait and
shaggy coat, it is a
highly distinctive
family pet.

OLD ENGLISH SHEEPDOG

*Immense coat
requires much
grooming*

*Coat colors are red,
sable, or black and
tan*

CORGI
There are two types of Corgis, the Pembroke
Welsh and the Cardigan Welsh, the latter
having a longer body than the former and
sporting a bushy, foxlike tail. Corgis (their
name comes from the Welsh *corci*
meaning dwarf dog), have been British
royal favorites since the days of
Richard the Lionhearted.

PEMBROKE
WELSH CORGI

Slightly sloping rump

Triangular, erect ears

Broad, deep chest

DUTCH SHEPHERD DOG

DUTCH SHEPHERD DOG
Little known outside the Netherlands, this superb working dog has served many purposes on the farm – guard, herder, and cart-puller. It originated in southern Holland at the beginning of the 19th century, with ancestry similar to that of the German Shepherd.

Velvety ears are half dropped

Eyes are round and alert

NEW ZEALAND HUNTAWAY

NEW ZEALAND HUNTAWAY
Unlike most other sheepdogs, this popular working dog keeps the flock moving and guides its direction by barking. Although not recognized by any kennel club, even in New Zealand, this 20th century dog breeds true as a herder.

AUSTRALIAN CATTLE DOG
Tough and courageous, this cattle-herding dog comes in two colors, red and blue (also known as Blue Heelers). Originally descended from English cattle dogs, the Australian Cattle Dog carries the genes of Red Bobtails, Collies, and Dingoes. By nature suspicious, this dog needs careful training.

Long, narrow head

RED CATTLE DOG

Harsh, dense overcoat

More livestock dogs

Wherever in the world they come from, livestock dogs are agile, quick-witted, all-weather types with plenty of sharp teeth to keep flocks moving! Where the terrain is rugged and hilly and distances are vast, dogs need great stamina to assist shepherds and cattlemen working on foot or on horseback.

MAREMMA SHEEPDOG

Very well known in Italy, the handsome, usually white Maremma is a reliable flock guard. It is a descendant of the white Eastern sheepdogs that spread across Europe 1,000 years ago. This majestic breed is highly intelligent but not easy to train.

Low-set tail is thickly feathered

MAREMMA SHEEPDOG

Distinctive white coat

Facial hair is finer textured

Hair forms long, wavy, strong locks

BERGAMASCO

Taking its name from Bergamo, the northern Italian province, this ancient but relatively unknown dog has a heavily corded coat to withstand weather and the kicks and butting of livestock. Courageous, agile, and friendly, it makes a superb sheepdog or watchdog, although it is not well suited to life in the city.

BERGAMASCO

KOMONDOR

Hungary's biggest sheepdog has been used since the 13th century to guard flocks from wolves, bears, and bandits. More recently this fiercely protective dog has proved effective in driving off marauding coyote packs in the US.

Coarse, insulating double coat

Muscular neck

AIDI

Prominent black nose

Corded coat that feels like felt

KOMONDOR

AIDI

The Aidi hails from Morocco where, for many centuries, it has guarded flocks of sheep and goats in the Atlas mountains. Sometimes it is used with the Sloughi to hunt game. The Aidi tracks it; the Sloughi seizes it.

HOVAWART

A 20th-century re-creation of the "Hofwarth," a dog that guarded the estates of the gentry in the Middle Ages, this German breed is rather dignified, and sometimes timid. With careful training it can make an obedient pet.

Smooth, dense coat has slight wave

HOVAWART

AUSTRALIAN KELPIE

Developed from collies in the 1800s, the work rate of this little sheepdog has become legendary. It is renowned for running across sheep's backs to get to the head of the flock and is the most common working sheepdog in Australia and New Zealand (above).

COLLIES

AFTER HUNTING DOGS, the earliest canines developed for a specific kind of work were shepherding types. In recent centuries, the collie family has represented the most admired and capable aspects of the dedicated working animal.

Small, triangular ears

Heavy mane

Dense, shiny topcoat

Small feet

BORDER COLLIE

BORDER COLLIE
Undoubtedly the smartest and most popular working dog in Britain, the Border Collie has a powerful herding instinct and aptitude bred into it over generations. Created in the 18th century on the moors of Scotland, this dog thrives on work and activity – so it is not an ideal city pet.

Hair naturally parts down middle of back

Ears largely covered with hair

Strong, well-boned forelegs

BEARDED COLLIE

BEARDED COLLIE
The origins of this exuberant, shaggy dog, sometimes called a Beardie, lie in medieval Britain. It is thought to have descended from Polish Lowland Sheepdogs brought to Scotland by visiting sailors. Although an industrious worker, it seems to adapt very well to being a family pet.

Nose is prone to sunburn

Long body

Pronounced frill between forelegs

ROUGH COLLIE

This beautiful and intelligent dog was a favorite of Queen Victoria of Britain. Royal approval rendered it a much-desired show dog in Britain and the US. In the 1940s, the breed gained international fame when a male called Pal was cast by Hollywood as Lassie (above).

ROUGH COLLIE

Small, semi-erect ears are close set

Long, harsh topcoat

SHETLAND SHEEPDOGS

Strongly resembling a Collie, this is an immensely popular dog, particularly in Japan, Britain, and the US. Its ancestors were either Rough Collies, or the Icelandic Yakkis that arrived in the Shetland Isles on whaling ships.

SMOOTH COLLIE

Essentially a Rough Collie with a smooth coat, this breed is less popular than the Rough and is seldom seen outside Britain. Sometimes Rough Collies produce a Smooth puppy in a litter but modern Smooth Collies are all derived from a tricolor pup called Trefoil, born in 1973. Although often shier than the Rough, it makes a fine pet.

Ears are erect; tips hang when dog is alert

Coat is short and dense

Muscular thighs

SMOOTH COLLIE

MOUNTAIN DOGS

WHEN COLD WINDS BLOW high up on isolated mountain slopes, gullies, and crags, special kinds of dogs come into their own. All mountain breeds are large, tough animals with weatherproof coats and abundant stamina.

ST BERNARD

Flews hang on short, square muzzle

Very muscular neck and shoulders

MOUNTAIN RESCUE
In the Alps, the St. Bernard has saved more than 2,500 lives over three centuries.

ST. BERNARD
This famous rescue dog was bred by monks of the Hospice of the Great Saint Bernard Pass. Working in teams of four, some dogs stayed with avalanche or exposure victims, licking their faces to help revive them, while others went to get help.

ESTRELA MOUNTAIN DOG

Since medieval times this breed, one of the oldest on the Iberian Peninsula, has defended flocks from wolves in the Estrela mountains of Portugal. Descended from ancient mastiffs, its dense, double coat protects it from harsh weather.

Rounded skull

Very powerful shoulders

ESTRELA MOUNTAIN DOG

BERNESE MOUNTAIN DOG

Soft, silky-textured coat, with good sheen

BERNESE MOUNTAIN DOG

Once a herder of livestock and puller of carts, this ancient breed had almost disappeared by the end of the last century. Today it is increasingly popular as a companion animal.

PYRENEAN MOUNTAIN DOG

A guardian of sheep in the Pyrenees since antiquity, this mighty dog was later used as a watchdog to protect French châteaux. King Louis XIV owned one at the Louvre palace in Paris.

Long, tapering, feathered tail

Hair on forelegs forms woolly "culottes"

PYRENEAN MOUNTAIN DOG

TATRA MOUNTAIN SHEEPDOG

Large, broad skull

TATRA MOUNTAIN SHEEPDOG

This herding and guarding dog comes from the Polish mountains. It stays with its sheep at all times and even has its thick, creamy white coat shorn with the sheep.

MASTIFFS

THESE LARGE AND POWERFUL dogs, usually with pendulous lips and drooping ears, are among the earliest canine types associated with humans. They were first depicted on Babylonian bas-reliefs. The name "mastiff" may come from the old French word "mestiff," meaning mongrel.

Broad skull with flat forehead

Forelegs are densely boned and set firmly apart

MASTIFF

Coat is fine, thick, and soft to the touch

SPANISH MASTIFF

Short feet are set firmly on the ground

PYRENEAN MASTIFF

This handsome Spanish dog guarded sheep flocks in the mountains between Spain and France. Four or five dogs, wearing spiked collars to protect their necks, would defend a flock of around 1,000 sheep against the once-common Pyrenean wolf.

SPANISH MASTIFF

This affable giant probably came to Spain with Phoenician and Greek traders 2,000 years ago. For centuries, it was employed to guard flocks from wolves. It is still used in the Pyrenees and is also a good companion.

PYRENEAN MASTIFF

Large head with slightly rounded skull

MASTIFF

Mastiffs in light armor, carrying spikes and cauldrons of flaming sulfur on their backs, were used in Roman warfare and, in the Middle Ages, against mounted knights. They also hunted wolves and took part in bearbaiting. The mastiff is normally loyal and gentle, but can be possessive.

Powerful hind legs

CHINESE SHAR-PEI

The name of this wrinkly skinned dog means sharkskin or sandpaper in Chinese. During Communist times, when dogs were prohibited, the breed almost died out. It was saved by a Hong Kong breeder who established stock in the US.

Prickly coat is oversized; hair stands on end

SHAR PEI

TIBETAN KYI APSO

Ears are fairly long

Long topcoat

Well-feathered tail has full curl

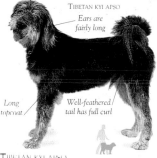

TIBETAN KYI APSO

The original function of this dog was to guard the homes and flocks of Tibetan shepherds. Its thick double coat provided insulation against harsh weather. Arriving in the West only recently, it is proving an excellent pet.

NEAPOLITAN MASTIFF

Heavy upper lips

NEAPOLITAN MASTIFF

This Italian giant can weigh over 220 lb (100 kg) and, though making a fearsome guard dog, can be good with children it knows. Its ancestry stretches back to the Molossus, a fighting dog of Classical times.

GUARD DOGS

BECAUSE OF their pack instinct, dogs warn other pack members of danger. Their fine sense of smell and hearing make them excellent guards. Specialized breeds of large, alert animals are quick to raise an alarm and attack intruders, if necessary.

No loose skin on elegant neck

GREAT DANE
Not so much Danish as German, this mighty but affectionate dog is descended from ancient mastiffs brought to northern Europe by the Roman legions. A similar type of dog appears on Greek coins of the 1st century B.C.

CERBERUS
In Greek mythology, the three-headed dog Cerberus, guarded the gateway to the Underworld.

Coarse, flat topcoat

ROTTWEILER
One of the strongest and most powerful dogs, the Rottweiler is a descendant of ancient boar hunters. Popular throughout the world as an efficient guard dog, it needs firm handling from an early age to temper its aggression.

ROTTWEILER

Long muzzle   BEAUCERON

BEAUCERON
A close relative of the Briard, this "King of Sheepdogs" is a brave and formidable guard dog, mistrustful of strangers. It originated in medieval France.

GREAT DANE

Long, tapering tail is prone to injuries at tip

Triangular, rather small ears that fold

Coat is medium length and evenly distributed

Hocks are set low

PORTUGUESE WATCH DOG

PORTUGUESE WATCH DOG
This old breed, descended from the Estrela Mountain Dog, is still employed to guard homes and farms in Portugal, and has also been used, with limited success, to control coyotes raiding sheep ranches in the US.

DOBERMAN PINSCHER

Flat top to skull

Small ears set high on head

CROPPING AND DOCKING

Ears cropped to make dog look fierce

Customarily docked tail

DOBERMAN PINSCHER
About 130 years ago, Louis Dobermann, a German tax inspector, crossed a variety of breeds (which he kept a secret) to create the ideal guard dog. This powerful animal was used by the German Army in World War I as a frontline patrol dog, and is used today by police across the world.

OTHER WORKING DOGS

NO OTHER ANIMAL is as eager to work alongside people as the dog. Cats make wonderful companions but, apart from catching the odd mouse, like an easy life. Horses have to be "broken" before they will work. Only the dog is a truly willing coworker – and able to shine in so many demanding roles.

NEWFOUNDLAND
The Vikings brought this big, bearlike dog to Newfoundland, Canada, in the 10th century. Strong and a powerful swimmer, it was used as a fisherman's assistant. In France, it is employed by the emergency services in sea rescues.

LANDSEER
In the US and Britain, the Landseer (above) is considered a color variety of the Newfoundland, while some countries classify it as a separate breed.

BRIARD

Muzzle is square, rather than round, with black nose

BRIARD
One of the best French sheepdogs, the Briard is a great runner, able to cover 50 miles (80 km) in a day. During World War I the French army used it to locate wounded soldiers, carry ammunition, and patrol the frontline.

Long, flexible, dry coat like that of a goat

NEWFOUNDLAND

Topcoat is flat, dense, and oily

THE "COACH DOG"

The Dalmatian was a fashionable carriage escort in the 18th century, acting as a deterrent against robbers on the road.

DALMATIAN

Distinctive, spotted coat

Ears taper to rounded tips

Feet are large and webbed

BOUVIER DES FLANDRES

This old and highly regarded Franco-Belgian breed was used as a guard dog, draft animal, and cattle herder. During World War I, it carried first-aid supplies for the French army.

BOUVIER DES FLANDRES

Large head is accentuated by mustache and beard

Topcoat is crisp to the touch

DALMATIAN

This elegant dog may have come to Europe, via Dalmatia, with gypsies traveling from north India in the Middle Ages. A relative of the pointer, it is active and intelligent.

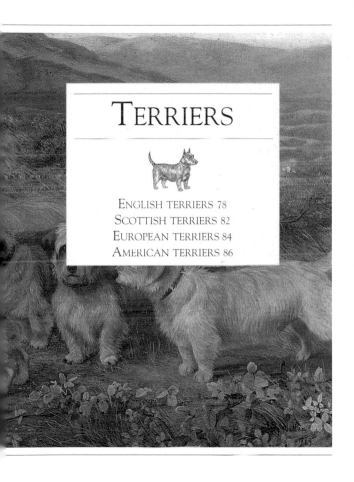

TERRIERS

ENGLISH TERRIERS

THE NAME "TERRIER" comes from the Latin word *terra*, meaning earth, and these dogs' ancestors specialized in earth work, running down into holes and burrows to confront rodents, foxes, or badgers.

AIREDALE TERRIER
The giant among terriers, this lively dog is named after the Yorkshire valley where it originated. It was developed in the 19th century by crossing the now-extinct Black and Tan Terrier with the Otterhound. It is a fine watchdog but has a tendency to get into street fights with other dogs!

Topline of ear fold is well above skull

Wiry, waterproof coat

FOX TERRIER

FOX TERRIER
The exuberant Fox Terrier comes in two forms, the Wire and the Smooth. Developed for fox-hunting, it carries the blood of Black and Tan Terriers, Beagles, Bulldogs, and even Greyhounds.

YORKSHIRE TERRIER

Hair is clipped on this specimen but can be very long

YORKSHIRE TERRIER
Now a toy, the dynamic "Yorkie" was developed about 100 years ago by working men in the North of England as a spirited ratter. The first Yorkshire Terriers were much bigger than today's delicate animals.

Hard, dense, wiry coat requires expert grooming for show purposes

AIREDALE TERRIER

Fringe of white, silky hair has been left unclipped

Thighs are muscular and powerful

BEDLINGTON TERRIER
Originating in the Northumberland coalfields in the 1800s, this dog may look like a lamb, but it is actually a determined and agile animal with a powerful bite. It was used for hunting rats, otters, foxes, and badgers.

Muscular hind legs

BEDLINGTON TERRIER

BORDER TERRIER
This tough little dog is a product of the rugged countryside on the Scottish borders and has altered little from its original form. It is small enough to follow a fox down a hole, but has long enough legs to keep up with riders on horseback.

Harsh, dense topcoat

BORDER TERRIER

JACK RUSSELL TERRIER
Very popular in Britain, and still very much a working dog, the robust Jack Russell was originally bred as a ratter. Its appearance varies, and the breed is not recognized.

PARSON JACK RUSSELL TERRIER
Developed by the Rev. John Russell in the 1800s, this type of Jack Russell is a recognized breed, has long legs, and used to hunt with horses.

More English terriers

Almost every region of England once had its own variety of terrier. Many varieties are now extinct. Some have been absorbed into other breeds, and others have achieved widespread recognition, if not for working then certainly in the show ring or as pets.

Small, V-shaped ears

MANCHESTER TERRIER
Once employed for rabbit coursing and ratting, the Manchester Terrier is a vivacious dog. It was first produced in Manchester, England, in the 1700s by crossing the now-extinct Black and Tan Terrier with the Whippet.

MANCHESTER TERRIER

Sleek coat

BULL TERRIER
This powerful, solidly built animal, with its origins in fighting dogs, was produced by crossing Bulldogs with terriers and later, English toy terriers and Whippets. Nowadays the Bull Terrier makes a gentle, affectionate dog if handled firmly.

Small, triangular eyes

Head curves down to nose

BULL TERRIER

STAFFORDSHIRE BULL TERRIER
Originating in Staffordshire, this well-muscled and exceedingly affectionate dog traces its ancestry to ferocious bullbaiters and agile terriers. It can be very aggressive toward other dogs.

Deep chest

STAFFORDSHIRE BULL TERRIER

Irish and Welsh terriers

For centuries, terriers have been popular among hunters working in the mountains and valleys of Ireland and Wales. In these lands a number of specific breeds were born.

KERRY
BLUE

_ Silky, bluish coat

KERRY BLUE TERRIER
This is the national dog of Ireland, used since the 18th century for fighting, hunting, herding, and house guarding. Ratting and rabbit hunting are still part of its working life.

SOFT-COATED WHEATEN TERRIER

Distinctive silky coat

SOFT-COATED WHEATEN TERRIER
The most ancient of the Irish breeds, its name derives from its coat, the color of ripening wheat. It is increasingly popular in the US.

WELSH TERRIER

Long hair on face gives square appearance

SEALYHAM TERRIER

Long neck

SEALYHAM TERRIER
The plucky Sealyham was first bred to accompany hounds hunting otter, badger and fox, its role being to go underground when necessary. It was developed at the Sealyham estate in Wales from 1850–1891.

WELSH TERRIER
Looking rather like a miniature Airedale, the Welsh Terrier is an indomitable character that was bred to hunt badger, otter, and fox. As a pet it needs firm handling and regular grooming.

SCOTTISH TERRIERS

Small, erect ears

CAIRN TERRIER

Docked tail

ALMOST ALL TERRIERS originated in the British Isles. Scotland is the home of some of the most famous and popular British breeds – a variety of fiesty badger-, rabbit- and rat-hunting terriers.

CAIRN TERRIER
The Cairn's name comes from the Gaelic word *cairn*, meaning a heap of stones. It was in such heaps, dotting the landscape of the Scottish Highlands, that these bright, quick-witted terriers would hunt rodents, weasels, foxes, and Scottish wild cats. The breed is equally at home in town and country and easier to train than many other terriers.

Profuse top coat with furry undercoat

Eyebrows are long and distinctive

SCOTTISH TERRIER
The reserved "Scottie" is, according to its devotees, the oldest breed native to Britain. It was certainly in the Scottish Highlands before the Roman invasion in A.D. 43. An independent-minded hunter of badger, fox, and vermin, its breed standard was set in 1883 and it is now a popular pet, particularly in the US.

Harsh, thick topcoat

SCOTTISH TERRIER

WEST HIGHLAND WHITE TERRIER

A tenacious little dog, the "Westie" was bred to hunt otter, fox, and vermin. Its ancestry is shared with the Scottish, Cairn, and Dandie Dinmont Terriers. Affectionate and perky, it makes a lively little guard dog.

Head is covered with thick hair

SCOTLAND'S MOST FAMOUS DOG

After Edinburgh policeman John Grey died in 1858, his ever-faithful Skye Terrier, Bobby, returned each day to Grey's grave until the dog himself died, 14 years later.

Erect ears are gracefully feathered

SKYE TERRIER

Feet have thick, black pads

WEST HIGHLAND
WHITE TERRIER

SKYE TERRIER

This breed may have originated in the 17th century when a Spanish galleon was wrecked off the coast of Skye in the Scottish Hebrides. On board were Maltese dogs that managed to get ashore and mate with the island dogs.

DANDIE DINMONT TERRIER

Taking its name from a dog-owning farmer in the novel *Guy Mannering* by Sir Walter Scott, this good-natured breed originated in 17th-century Scottish border country. Once a hunter of otter and badger, it is now a charming pet.

DANDIE
DINMONT

Large skull with domed forehead

EUROPEAN TERRIERS

TERRIERS WERE EXPORTED from the British Isles and Ireland to continental Europe, where countries developed their own terrier breeds. Each was suited for particular work or terrain, and had a distinctive appearance.

Long, powerful jaws

High-set tail has been docked

Angle on hind legs allows for speed

MINIATURE SCHNAUZER

MINIATURE SCHNAUZER
Once employed as an expert rat catcher, this dog is a diminutive version of the Giant and Standard Schnauzers, with the addition of Affenpinscher and Miniature Pinscher blood. It has an amiable temperament.

Long hair forms fringe around face

Large, round eyes

GRIFFON BRUXELLOIS
This Belgian dog is a classic "Euro-dog" as it carries the genes of German Affenpinschers, French Barbets, Yorkshire Terriers, and Dutch Smoushonds. Its original use was as a rat catcher in stables. The Petit Brabancon is a smooth-coated variety of the Griffon Bruxellois.

PETIT BRABANCON

GRIFFON BRUXELLOIS

AFFENPINSCHER

Its name means "monkey terrier" in Germany where this zestful little dog originated, and it does have a flat, monkeylike face. Although it is now normally a pet, it is still good at ratting and at tracking rabbits.

Dark eyes have bushy brows

Broad chest is covered with dense hair

AFFENPINSCHER

GERMAN PINSCHER

This dog originated in 18th-century Germany and is now rather rare. A multipurpose farmer's dog, it was the forebear of the Miniature Pinscher and Doberman. It needs firm handling, but can be loyal.

Body is robust and well muscled

Short coat is smooth and glossy

GERMAN PINSCHER

DUTCH SMOUSHOND

This tough little terrier was very popular at the end of the last century as a gentleman's companion, but its numbers later declined until it was almost extinct by the end of World War 1. The breed was revived by selective breeding in the 1970s.

Long, wispy hair

Protective guard hair and down

DUTCH SMOUSHOND

Prominent nose

CZESKY TERRIER

CZESKY TERRIER

The Czesky may look unusual, but it is a typical feisty terrier developed in the 1940s from Scottish, Sealyham and, possibly, Dandie Dinmont Terriers.

AMERICAN TERRIERS

SOON AFTER REACHING THE NEW WORLD,
terriers evolved into some of the relatively
few wholly American breeds. Some were
developed for fighting; others
were miniaturized to produce
successful companions.

AMERICAN TOY TERRIER
Developed in the 1930s by crossing Smooth
Fox Terriers with English Toy Terriers and
Chihuahuas, this is an expert ratter with
all the enthusiasm and determination of
its Fox Terrier ancestors. It also makes a
fine family pet and can be trained as an
efficient hearing dog for deaf people.

*Square
body shape*

AMERICAN TOY TERRIER

*Large, batlike
ears*

*Short, smooth
coat*

19TH-CENTURY BOSTON

*Small, rounded
feet with well-
arched toes*

BOSTON TERRIER

BOSTON TERRIER
This boisterous and intelligent terrier
was developed in 19th-century
Boston for the "sport" of dogfighting
by crossing Bulldogs with Bull
Terriers, but it no longer has a
taste for violence.

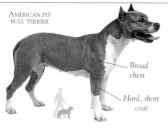

AMERICAN PIT
BULL TERRIER

Broad
chest

Hard, short
coat

AMERICAN STAFFORDSHIRE TERRIER
Selectively bred from British Staffordshire
Bull Terriers, this dog is taller, heavier,
and bulkier than the latter. It can be very
loyal and affectionate with humans while
fiercely hostile toward
other animals.

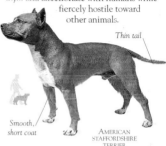

Thin tail

Smooth,
short coat

AMERICAN
STAFFORDSHIRE
TERRIER

AMERICAN PIT BULL TERRIER
A descendant of the Staffordshire Bull
Terrier and other fighting dogs, the Pit
Bull is now banned in some countries
because of its aggressive nature. However,
it can be an obedient companion if
handled firmly from puppyhood.

Australian terriers

In the 1800s, settlers brought terriers to Australia.
Originally they were ratters on farms and
homesteads, later they became companions.

AUSTRALIAN
TERRIER

AUSTRALIAN SILKY TERRIER
A product of Australian
and Yorkshire Terriers,
this pretty little animal,
once known as the
"Sydney Silky" after its
birthplace, was never
a working dog.

AUSTRALIAN
SILKY TERRIER

AUSTRALIAN TERRIER
This brave and bouncy little Australian
dog earns its keep on farms in the outback
where it kills snakes and vermin and is a
reliable watchdog. The Cairn, Yorkshire,
Skye, and perhaps the Norwich Terrier
are its ancestors.

SPECIAL BREEDS AND TOY DOGS

BULLDOGS AND BOXERS

THE BULLENBEISSER ("bull biter") was a medieval German hunting dog whose forebears were the mastiff types of Classical times. When the baiting of bulls and other dangerous animals became a "sport," a small Bullenbeisser, the Brabanter, came into fashion. Both the bulldog and boxer are descended from this dog.

Very short, broad nose

BULLDOG

Undershot lower jaw

Extremely wide chest

BEST OF BRITISH
The Bulldog is a British national symbol, portraying strength and stubbornness.

BULLDOG
With the demise of British bull-baiting in 1835, this ferocious breed was in danger of extinction. Bill George, a breeder, transformed it into its present, less aggressive form. It is now one of the more kindly breeds.

FRENCH BULLDOG

The "Frenchie" is a lively and devoted family pet, that also makes a fine watchdog. As its name suggests, it originated in France in the 1860s when English lace makers arrived on the Normandy coast. They brought with them small English Bulldogs, some of which weighed no more than 10 lb (4.5 kg).

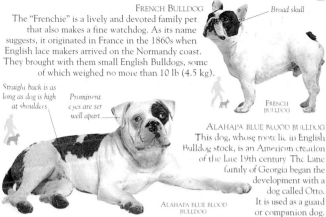

Broad skull

FRENCH BULLDOG

Straight back is as long as dog is high at shoulders

Prominent eyes are set well apart

ALAHAPA BLUE BLOOD BULLDOG

ALAHAPA BLUE BLOOD BULLDOG

This dog, whose roots lie in English Bulldog stock, is an American creation of the late 19th century. The Lane family of Georgia began the development with a dog called Otto. It is used as a guard or companion dog.

BULL BOXER

THE BULL BOXER

A cross between a Boxer and a Staffordshire Bull Terrier, this dog possesses the best features of both. Developed in the 1990s in Britain, the attractive Bull Boxer is bright and fun-loving.

BOXER

Virtually unknown outside Germany until the end of World War II, Boxers are now highly popular as family pets and guard dogs across the world. Blessed with boundless energy, they demand plenty of exercise.

Strong, muscular neck without dewlap

Powerful thighs

Well-arched ribs

BOXER

SPITZES

THESE ARE DOGS OF THE NORTH, descendants of canines that migrated to Arctic regions thousands of years ago, interbred with wolves, and later moved south again into temperate regions. Arguably, the relationship between spitz and human has been closer than that of any other type of dog.

Medium-sized, triangular ears

Medium-length muzzle

SIBERIAN HUSKY
This superb sled-dog was developed by the Chukchi, Inuit nomads of Siberia, and was brought to North America about 100 years ago. Amazingly tough, yet amiable, it is equally happy herding reindeer, pulling sleds, or guarding.

Tail is bushy and needs grooming during shedding season

SIBERIAN HUSKY

Brown, almond-shaped eyes

ALASKAN MALAMUTE
Records of the first European settlers in North America mention this dog which takes its name from an Inuit people. After Alaska was ceded to the US by Russia in 1867, the breed nearly disappeared, but in the 1920s steps were taken to preserve it.

White coloration on lower body

ALASKAN MALAMUTE

CHOW CHOW

The Chow Chow's meat was once a delicacy in Mongolia and Manchuria, and its skin a popular fur for clothing. It was also used as a guard dog, for pulling carts, and for hunting. The Chow Chow and the Shar-Pei are the only dogs with black-pigmented tongues.

Small ears blend with the ruff

Muzzle is broad along its length

CHOW CHOW

ESKIMO DOG

Dense coat protects dog from freezing temperatures

Classic spitz curl in tail

ESKIMO DOG

Originating in Canada, this hardy, energetic breed was the only means of transportation for the Hudson Bay Inuit for thousands of years. Essentially a pack dog with a tendency to squabble for seniority, it makes a better working dog than companion.

NORWEGIAN ELKHOUND

A classic spitz breed and the national dog of Norway, this dog has existed in Scandinavia for at least 5,000 years. It has hunted lynx and wolf, as well as elk, and is a successful retriever of small game. Norwegian farmers also use it to herd chickens.

Thick, coarse topcoat

NORWEGIAN ELKHOUND

Strong, thick neck

JAPANESE AKITA

Sturdy, powerful legs

JAPANESE AKITA

The largest of the Japanese spitz types, the Akita was originally used for hunting deer, boar, and bear, as well as for the "sport" of dogfighting, now illegal in Japan. Courageous and loyal, it can make a fine house dog but needs firm handling.

More spitzes

The original spitz breeds were important for human survival in northern regions, but as time went by, types suited to milder climates and gentler conditions were developed. They were employed for a variety of different tasks.

Tail curves vigorously

Distinctive red coat

FINNISH SPITZ

FINNISH SPITZ
Once a fearless hunter of bear and other game in Finland, this ancient spitz is now a bird dog used for flushing wood grouse. Cheerful, lively, and loyal, it is excellent with children.

Densely furred, small, triangular ears

VOLPINO

KEESHOND
A typical spitz-type breed from Holland, the Keeshond was once widely used as a guard dog on canal boats. It may be named after Kees de Gyselaer, a Dutch politician who owned one of these dogs.

Profuse coat in ruff around neck

KEESHOND

VOLPINO
This elegant dog is usually white and weighs 9–11 lb (4–5 kg). Volpinos were popular as pets in Renaissance Italy, and ladies often decorated them with bracelets of ivory. Today, the Volpino makes a good companion and watchdog.

POMERANIAN

Though now a diminutive "toy," the ancestors of this breed pulled sleds in the Arctic. Queen Victoria of Britain first saw white Pomeranians in Florence in 1888, and soon became an enthusiastic owner.

Very long, bushy tail

SAMOYED

Ruff is typical of all Arctic spitz breeds

POMERANIAN

SAMOYED

Named after a Siberian nomadic people, this very affectionate, intelligent, and active dog has accompanied Polar explorers on their expeditions. Once a multicolored breed, it is now white, white and beige, or cream in color.

Coat is longest around neck

Dense feathering of hair

PAPILLON

Dainty, with butterflylike ears, the shape and coat of this dog originates from bigger spitz types of the north. One of Europe's oldest breeds, its more recent ancestors were Dwarf Spaniels brought to 16th-century Spain from China.

Ears carried obliquely, like a butterfly's wings

SCHIPPERKE

PAPILLON

SCHIPPERKE

Its name means "little captain" or "boatman" in Flemish and for centuries this robust little dog, descended from the Northern Spitz, worked as guard and rat-catcher on the canal boats of Flanders.

Cords provide insulating layer

CORDED POODLE
The Standard and, later, the Medium, Miniature, and Toy Poodles, were developed from this now-rare breed. Natural selection produced the coat, which guards against hostile weather.

POODLES

ONE OF THE BEST-LOVED BREEDS, the poodle is much more than just a pretty creature with a distinctive haircut. Descended from ancient water dogs and water spaniels, its name is derived from the German "pudel," meaning "one who splashes in water."

Dignified head

Hair left on tail gives buoyancy

Hair on feet increases buoyancy

STANDARD POODLE

STANDARD POODLE
The Standard is still in essence a working dog, designed as a wildfowl retriever. Originally, poodle clipping was not cosmetic, but was done in order to protect joints and vital organs from cold water.

DOGGY BAG
Sometimes regarded as fashion items, poodles may be seen wearing clothing, jewelry, even nail polish!

Frizzy hair

MINIATURE POODLE

TOY POODLE

MINIATURE AND TOY POODLES
These dogs are the product of selective breeding aimed at developing scaled-down poodles that are intelligent, lively, and loving companions.

Long, straight muzzle

MEDIUM POODLE

Straight, solid legs

MEDIUM POODLE
In some countries, Medium Poodles are recognized as a separate breed. They are midway in size between the Standard and Miniature types, but in other ways identical.

TYPES OF CLIP

PUPPY CLIP	DUTCH CLIP	LAMB CLIP	LION CLIP

GROOMING AND CLIPPING
Nowadays poodles are clipped for fashion and the show bench. The classic poodle clip is the European "Lion" style. Other styles include the "Dutch" Clip, the "Lamb" Clip, and, for puppies up to one year, the "Puppy" Clip.

BEFORE

Coat tightly clipped

Profuse, frizzy coat

Ears are clipped and sculptured

AFTER

BICHON FRISÉ

EUROPEAN TOY DOGS

CONVENIENT-SIZED and aesthetically pleasing, toy dogs represent the extreme of selective breeding; their ancestors were much bigger dogs. The term "toy," which has been applied to dogs since 1863, does not mean "plaything" but simply "diminutive."

White, frizzy hair

Strong, straight legs

BOLOGNESE
Resembling the Maltese and a cousin of the Bichon Frisé, the Bolognese is still rare in its native Italy. It originated in the 13th century, possibly from Bichons of southern Italy. Its white, fluffy, fine coat protects it from the heat of Italian summers. Rather shy, it nevertheless makes a fine companion.

Ears set wide, giving square appearance

BOLOGNESE

Profuse, silky hair

BICHON FRISÉ
Adaptable and lively, the Bichon has found a large following since its emergence from obscurity in the 1970s. It probably originated in the Canary Islands and came to Europe with sailors in the 14th century.

MALTESE

This sweet-natured breed originated in Malta, or in the Sicilian town of Melita. Statues of similar dogs have been found in Egyptian tombs of 1300 B.C. Today's Maltese may be descended from spaniels and poodles.

Luxurious coat needs regular grooming

MALTESE

MINIATURE PINSCHER

Large, round eyes

Almost unknown outside Germany before 1900, this athletic dog has become universally popular, particularly in the US. A lively animal, it has a distinctive high-stepping gait and makes a good pet.

MINIATURE PINSCHER

LOWCHEN

A French breed with a German name (meaning "little lion"), this dog has a similar ancestry to the Bichon and Maltese. Sometimes willful, the Lowchen makes a good house dog and only need be given the "lion clip" for show purposes

Pointed ears are covered with dense hair

Long, silky hair

HAVANESE

Plume of hair

Delicate, wavy coat

LOWCHEN

HAVANESE

A descendant of the Maltese or Bolognese crossed with poodles, the Havanese was developed in Cuba in the 18th and 19th centuries and is increasingly popular in the US. This gentle, sometimes shy dog is good with children.

ORIENTAL TOY DOGS

IN ANCIENT ORIENTAL civilizations, toy dogs were greatly esteemed, even considered sacred. Pampered by the nobility and priesthood and small enough to lie inside the sleeves of their masters' robes, they were often called "sleeve dogs."

JAPANESE FU DOG
An image of the mythical Fu Dog was a good luck talisman.

PEKINGESE
This sacred dog of the Chinese Imperial House was venerated as an embodiment of the mythical Fu Dog that drove off evil spirits. Commoners had to bow to it, and stealing one was punishable by death. It came to the West after 1860, when British soldiers captured the Emperor's Summer Palace during the Opium Wars.

Long, silky coat

Nose is snub and broad

PEKINGESE

Round face and flat muzzle

PUG
Pug is an old English word for goblin or monkey that was given to this friendly breed in the late 18th century. Many experts believe it is descended from a short-haired relative of the Pekingese; others claim it to be the product of small Bulldogs or a miniature form of the rare French Mastiff.

PUG

JAPANESE CHIN
Resembling the Pekingese, this dog is probably descended from the Tibetan Spaniel. A perfect house pet, it arrived in Europe in the 17th century, when Portuguese sailors presented some Chins to Princess Catalina de Braganza.

Miniaturization has produced a peculiar skull shape

JAPANESE CHIN SKULL

Tail has dense, feathered hair

JAPANESE CHIN

LHASA APSO

Feathered ears cover face

LHASA APSO
While the name "Lhasa" probably refers to the capital of Tibet, "apso" may mean "goatlike" – a reference to this breed's long, coarse coat. This ancient breed was, for centuries, rarely permitted to leave Tibet. The few that did were gifts from the Dalai Lama to honored guests.

Long parting from back of head

Wispy hair on ears

Skin may be plain or spotted

CHINESE CRESTED DOG
Contrary to its name, this curious breed may have originated in Africa and been taken to Asia by traders. The hairless types tend to show genetic defects when breeding. Fortunately, they often have coated pups, "Powder Puffs," that are stronger genetically.

Square, compact body

CHINESE CRESTED DOG

SOUTHERN AMERICAN TOYS

IT IS SOMETIMES HARD to imagine that these diminutive, ornamental, even bizarre toy dogs of Latin America are descended, like other breeds, from the wolf, and not, as some people believe, from crosses with rabbits!

Small, neat mouth prone to tooth loss

Long coat is rarer than the short coat

SMOOTH-COATED CHIHUAHUA
Descended perhaps from dogs held sacred by the Incas and Aztecs, the antecedents of the Chihuahua are still a matter of debate. Some experts think they arrived with the Spanish *conquistadores*; others believe that the Chinese brought them to the Americas long before.

SMOOTH-COATED
CHIHUAHUA

Heavy fringe of hair on ears

LONG-COATED
CHIHUAHUA
This breed comes in two forms, the Smooth-coated and Long-haired, which are otherwise identical. The Aztecs had no wool or cotton, but made cloth from the hair of Chihuahua-type dogs.

LONG-COATED CHIHUAHUA

PERUVIAN INCA ORCHID
This almost hairless dog was first seen by the *conquistadores* in the homes of Inca nobility in the early 16th century. It makes a friendly companion, but is prone to skin, eye, and dental problems.

Hair grows on top of head

White or pink skin is prone to sunburn

PERUVIAN INCA ORCHID

MOTHER WITH PUPS
This pottery jar of the Chimu culture of Peru (c.AD 1000–1500) features Chihuahua-type dogs.

Skin needs oiling to prevent burning by sun

INCA HAIRLESS DOG

MINIATURE MEXICAN HAIRLESS
The forebears of this miniaturized form of the Standard Mexican Hairless were, like those of other hairless dogs, genetic "freaks." About one in three puppies partially revert to type and have downy fur.

Erect ears have been developed to refine hearing

Skin feels hot to the touch because of dog's high temperature

INCA HAIRLESS DOG
This dog was developed in three sizes by the Incas of Peru; small ones were used as bed warmers, medium and large ones for hunting. They may have evolved in the Americas from the Timber Wolf or have been introduced before the Spanish conquest, from Asia, Polynesia, or Africa.

MINIATURE MEXICAN HAIRLESS

MINIATURE SPANIELS

ALTHOUGH THE WORD
"spaniel" has its origin in
Spain, some dogs classed
as spaniels have ancestries
rooted far from the Iberian
Peninsula. These include
miniature spaniels, which
have long made popular
companions, especially
with royalty.

CAVALIER KING
CHARLES SPANIEL

*Slight wave in
long hair*

KING CHARLES
SPANIEL PUPPY

*Short, broad
back and deep
chest*

KING CHARLES SPANIEL
Charles II of England, Scotland, and
Ireland (1660–85), after whom this breed
is named, adored spaniels, kept some in
his Whitehall palace and, it was said,
neglected affairs of state to play with them.

CHARLES II WITH HIS BROTHER AND SISTER

104

CAVALIER KING CHARLES SPANIEL

During the 1920s, crossbreeding led to the creation of this breed, which is slightly larger than the King Charles spaniel, with a flatter skull and longer muzzle. It was an attempt to revert back to the type of spaniel of which Charles II was so fond.

PRINCE CHARLES SPANIEL

Pearly white coat with black and tan markings

Long, silky coat has slight wave, no curl

PRINCE CHARLES SPANIEL

One variety of King Charles is the Prince Charles. It has a white coat and black and tan markings. Others are the Black and Tan, the Blenheim, and the Ruby.

White coat with chestnut patches

BLENHEIM KING CHARLES SPANIEL

TIBETAN SPANIEL

BLENHEIM KING CHARLES SPANIEL

The Blenheim is a variety of King Charles Spaniel with a white coat and chestnut markings. Ladies of the royal court kept small spaniels under their voluminous skirts to provide warmth in winter.

This ancient breed, probably the forebear of the Japanese Chin, somewhat resembles the Pekingese. It was once used by Tibetan monks to turn their prayer wheels. A healthier breed overall than the Pekingese, it makes a first-class companion.

REFERENCE SECTION

KENNEL CLUB BREED LIST

The following breeds and breed groupings are recognized by the American Kennel Club (AKC):

SPORTING GROUP
Brittanys
Pointers
Pointers, German Shorthaired
Pointers, German Wirehaired
Retrievers, Chesapeake Bay
Retrievers, Curly-Coated
Retrievers, Flat-Coated
Retrievers, Golden
Retrievers, Labrador
Setters, English
Setters, Gordon
Setters, Irish
Spaniels, American Water
Spaniels, Clumber
Spaniels, Cocker
Spaniels, English Cocker
Spaniels, English Springer
Spaniels, Field
Spaniels, Irish Water
Spaniels, Sussex
Spaniels, Welsh Springer
Vizslas
Weimaraners
Wirehaired Pointing Griffons

HOUND GROUP
Afghan Hounds
Basenjis
Basset Hounds
Beagles
Black and Tan Coonhounds
Bloodhounds
Borzois
Dachshunds
Foxhounds, American
Foxhounds, English
Greyhounds
Harriers
Ibizan Hounds
Irish Wolfhounds
Norwegian Elkhounds
Otterhounds
Petits Bassets Griffons Vendéens
Pharaoh Hounds
Rhodesian Ridgebacks
Salukis
Scottish Deerhounds
Whippets

WORKING GROUP
Akitas
Alaskan Malamutes
Anatolian Shepherds
Bernese Mountain Dogs
Boxers
Bullmastiffs
Doberman Pinschers
German Pinschers
Giant Schnauzers
Great Danes
Great Pyrenees
Greater Swiss Mountain Dog
Komondorok
Kuvaszok
Mastiffs
Newfoundlands
Portuguese Water Dogs
Rottweilers
Saint Bernards
Samoyeds
Siberian Huskies
Standard Schnauzers

TERRIER GROUP
Airedale Terriers
American Staffordshire Terriers
Australian Terriers
Bedlington Terriers
Border Terriers
Bull Terriers
Cairn Terriers
Dandie Dinmont Terriers
Fox Terriers (Smooth)
Fox Terriers (Wire)
Irish Terriers
Kerry Blue Terriers
Lakeland Terriers
Manchester Terriers (Standard)
Miniature Bull Terriers
Miniature Schnauzers
Norfolk Terriers
Norwich Terriers
Scottish Terriers
Sealyham Terriers
Skye Terriers
Smooth Fox Terriers
Soft-Coated Wheaten Terriers
Staffordshire Bull Terriers
Welsh Terriers

West Highland White
Terriers

NONSPORTING GROUP
American Eskimo Dogs
Bichons Frises
Boston Terriers
Bulldogs
Chinese Shar-Peis
Chow Chows
Dalmatians
Finnish Spitz
French Bulldogs
Keeshonden
Lhasa Apsos
Löwchens
Poodles
Schipperkes
Shiba Inus
Tibetan Spaniels
Tibetan Terriers

TOY GROUP
Affenpinschers
Brussels Griffons
Cavalier King Charles
Spaniels
Chihuahuas
Chinese Cresteds
English Toy Spaniels
Havaneses
Italian Greyhounds
Japanese Chin
Maltese
Manchester Terriers
Miniature Pinschers
Papillons
Pekingese
Pomeranians
Poodles
Pugs
Shih Tzu

Silky Terriers
Toy Fox Terriers
Yorkshire Terriers

HERDING GROUP
Australian Cattle Dogs
Australian Shepherds
Bearded Collies
Belgian Malinois
Belgian Sheepdogs
Belgian Tervuren
Border Collie
Bouviers des Flandres
Briards
Canaan Dogs
Collies
German Shepherd Dogs
Old English Sheepdogs
Polish Lowland
Sheepdogs
Pulis
Shetland Sheepdogs
Welsh Corgis, Cardigan
Welsh Corgis, Pembroke

MISCELLANEOUS
Beaucerons
Black Russian Terriers
Glen of Imaal Terriers
Neapolitan Mastiffs
Nova Scotia Duck Tolling
Retrievers
Plott Hounds
Redbone Coonhounds

To register a dog, contact the
AKC at the following address:
American Kennel Club
Customer Service
5580 Centerview Drive
Raleigh, NC 27606
(919)233-9767

THE AMERICAN KENNEL CLUB
The AKC was founded in 1884
for the purpose of studying,
breeding, exhibiting, and
improving purebred dogs. To be
recognized, a breed must have a
national club that promotes its
interest, a written breed
standard (a document
describing the ideal qualities of
the breed), and a diverse gene
pool consisting of at least
300–400 dogs owned by
different people living in
various parts of the US. For
developing breeds seeking
recognition, acceptance in the
Miscellaneous category, usually
for one to three years, allows
for familiarization prior to full
recognition.

CHOOSING A DOG

TAKING ON THE RESPONSIBILITY of
owning a dog, with all its rewards,
demands careful thought. The main
factors to consider are health, appearance,
character, and size of the adult dog. Choose
a pet that is right for your lifestyle.

HANDLING
A PUPPY

*If a puppy is
relaxed when
picked up it
might be an
easygoing adult*

*Eyes bright
and free from
discharge*

POINTS TO CHECK

*Coat free
from lice or
fleas*

CHOOSING A PUPPY
Select a pup that is alert and sociable.
Generally speaking, males are likely to
be more active and headstrong while
females are easier to train but demand
more affection. Be prepared to give a pup
constant attention and house training.

*Teeth
correctly
aligned*

PEDIGREE POODLE

*Check for
presence of
dewclaws*

PEDIGREE OR MONGREL?
With a purebred you can be fairly sure of the
dog's ultimate size and behavior. Mongrels are
more often in need of a good home, can be
delightful companions, and are less prone to
hereditary diseases. But they can be something
of an unknown quantity.

BIG OR SMALL?

Generally, large breeds do not live as long as small breeds. Great Danes seldom pass 12 years of age; some terriers reach 20. Big dogs need more space, exercise, and food than little ones. Some small breeds can be fickle with food and surprisingly snappy. Ideal for compact homes, these breeds still need physical and mental exercise.

IRISH WOLFHOUND AND WIRE-HAIRED DACHSHUND

Body well proportioned

Clean anal area. No diarrhea

VACCINATION

INOCULATIONS

Ideally, a pet should have been vaccinated against major diseases before you obtain it, and have a certificate to prove it. Pups should not leave their mothers before eight weeks of age.

Male should have two testicles

Pot belly may indicate worms

DOGS FROM SHELTERS

SHELTERS

If you are a fairly experienced dog owner, obtain a dog from a shelter; you may well save its life. The shelter should arrange a veterinary checkup of the dog before parting with it. These dogs can take a while to settle down in new homes.

CARING FOR A DOG

OWNING A DOG is a 365-day-a-year responsibility and privilege. Ongoing care and supervision of the animal has to be provided. The essentials are good housing, an adequate, balanced diet, regular exercise, and grooming, during which the condition of the body can be checked.

FEEDING

There are three main types of balanced diet: dry (complete), canned (some need cereal supplement), and semimoist (complete). These are more reliable nutritionally than your own mix of meat, scraps, or biscuits.

DAILY FEEDING OF AN ADULT DOG*	
DOG TYPE	CALORIES
TOY 11 LB (5 KG) (YORKSHIRE TERRIER)	210
SMALL 22 LB (10 KG) (WEST HIGHLAND TERRIER)	590
MEDIUM 66 LB (30 KG) (SPRINGER SPANIEL)	900
LARGE 88 LB (40 KG) (GERMAN SHEPHERD)	1,680
GIANT 176 LB (80 KG) (GREAT DANE)	2,800

*These figures are an approximate guide only.

TYPES OF DOG FOOD

SEMIMOIST CEREALS

BISCUITS TREATS

FOOD AND WATER BOWLS

BASIC EQUIPMENT

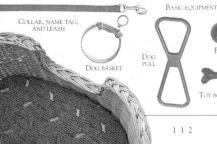

COLLAR, NAME TAG, AND LEASH

DOG BASKET

DOG PULL

BALL

TOY BONE

TOYS

Toys satisfy a dog's natural desires to chase, chew, and tug. They exercise a dog's mind as well as teeth, assist puppies' physical and social development, and create a bond between owner and pet.

TRIMMING NAILS

NAIL CLIPPERS

Dogs' nails can be clipped with a "guillotine" clipper. If you can't see the "quick" in a black nail, ask your vet to do the clipping.

Avoid "quick" in nail

WHERE TO CUT NAIL

"Quick"

Nail

Cutting line

GROOMING

Grooming, while essential for some coat types, must be provided for all dogs (even the Mexican Hairless!) It stimulates skin health, helps control parasite invasion, and helps your dog look and feel good. For grooming, a few inexpensive tools are needed.

GROOMING EQUIPMENT

Flea comb

Double-headed brush for finishing

Wire comb for untangling

TYPES OF COAT

LONG COATS
German Shepherd, Collie, Newfoundland, Old English Sheepdog, Spitzes. Daily brushing. Twice yearly bathing. Clip Old English to 1 in (2.5 cm).

SILKY COATS
Afghan, Yorkie, Lhasa Apso, setters, Pekingese, spaniels. Daily brush and comb. Strip and bathe setter, Afghan, spaniel every 3 months. Trim Yorkie.

SHORT COATS
Smooth-haired Dachshund, Labrador, Whippet, Boxer, Corgi. Easiest to groom (daily to weekly). Bathe when dirty. Some breeds shed in summer.

CURLY NONSHEDDING
Bedlington, poodles, Kerry Blue. These don't shed, so clip and bathe every 6–8 weeks. Brush every 2 days. Trim excess hair in ear canals.

WIRE-HAIRED
Most terriers, Wire-haired Dachshund, Schnauzers. Daily combing. Strip top coat and bathe every 3–4 months or clip every 6–8 weeks.

UNUSUAL COATS
The little bit of hair on the Mexican Hairless and Chinese Crested needs regular combing. Puli and Komondor need special attention, including oiling.

HOME NURSING

Collar prevents self-mutilation and bandage removal

WHEN A PET GETS SICK it is wise to seek professional advice from a vet without delay. Only rely on a pharmacist or pet shop for very minor ailments. At such times an owner should be prepared to nurse the dog back to health. Here are some important procedures to bear in mind.

GIVING MEDICINE

Pour liquid medicine into a "pouch," formed by gently pulling out the lower lip. Allow the dog to open its mouth and swallow between each spoonful.

Few medicines are pleasant-tasting – you may encounter resistance

NURSING A SICK DOG

Rest, warmth, and good ventilation are essential when nursing all sick dogs. Unless your vet advises otherwise, give nourishing liquids (honey or glucose and water or human invalid food) frequently in small quantities; if necessary, spoonfeed.

EMPTYING ANAL GLANDS

A dog's anal glands can get blocked, causing irritation. Unblock them by placing a cotton ball over the anus and firmly squeezing with thumb and index finger on either side. Your vet can show you how.

TAKING TEMPERATURE

A dog's temperature is taken by placing a clinical thermometer (a stubby ended glass one, or better, an unbreakable, electronic kind), in the rectum for 30 seconds. The normal temperature for a dog is 100.4–102.2° F (38–39°C) .

EAR DROPS

Hold the ear flap and steady the head. Introduce the drops into the ears and allow it to run down. Massage the ear canal from the outside and then stand back or your pet will probably shake any excess drops over you.

BRUSHING TEETH

To prevent gum and tooth disease, it is wise to check a dog's teeth and gums once a week. Brush your dog's teeth daily using its own toothbrush, salt and water, or, better still, a special canine toothpaste obtainable from a vet or pet store.

EYEDROPS AND OINTMENTS

Hold the eye open with finger and thumb. Keep the eyedropper parallel with, not pointed at, the eye and allow the medication to fall directly onto the cornea or into the pink conjunctival sac. Hold the eyelids closed for a second or two.

FIRST AID

CANINE ACCIDENTS OCCUR more often outside than
inside the home. If an animal is injured, don't panic.
Telephone the vet for advice after first assessing the
problem. Then take the dog to the vet, if medical
treatment is required.

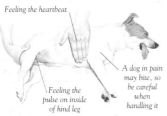

Feeling the heartbeat

*A dog in pain
may bite, so
be careful
when
handling it*

*Feeling the
pulse on inside
of hind leg*

ASSESSING AN INJURED DOG
Approach cautiously and speak softly to
the dog. Restrain gently with improvised
leash and muzzle. Ensure that the dog
isn't trapped. Look for heartbeat (left
side of chest), breathing, major bleeding,
gasping, pale gums, inability to stand,
and fractures. If the wound is bleeding,
apply pressure, then bandage it.

MOVING AN INJURED DOG

1 Muzzle the dog, if necessary. Transfer
the dog onto a blanket, which acts
as a sling and can be slid underneath it.
Move gently, preferably with two helpers
to support head, back, and pelvis.

2 Hold the blanket taut between two
people, with the third supporting
the dog's back, and maneuver the dog
carefully into the car. Make sure
someone sits with it during the trip.

RESTRAINING A DOG
Less seriously injured dogs need restraining for treatment. Small dogs should be held tightly around the collar. Medium-sized dogs are held as in the illustration; large dogs need two people.

Use round-ended tweezers

Helper restrains dog

MAKING A MUZZLE
Use a tie, bandage or rope. Make a loop, knot it under and then over the muzzle, and tie the ends behind the ears. Never muzzle short-nosed dogs or those with breathing problems.

CHOKING
Restrain the dog and open its mouth as if giving a pill. Carefully remove the foreign body with fingers, tweezers, or fine pliers.

Keep dog calm

BANDAGING WOUNDS
Don't apply medication before a vet has examined a wound. Close the wound and apply a gauze pad, or clean cloth, NOT a cotton ball. Wrap elastic bandage round 4–5 times. Anchor on other body parts. Secure with adhesive tape, NOT rubber bands.

Bandage protects from further damage

ARTIFICIAL RESPIRATION
Check that the airway is clear, and the mouth is open with tongue forwards. Place both hands flat on chest (one hand for toy breeds) over rib area and push down firmly. Release pressure immediately. Repeat at 5-second intervals.

If heart is beating, breathe into nostrils to inflate lungs

If heart is not beating, start cardiac massage

RESUSCITATION

CARDIAC MASSAGE

AMAZING DOGS

There are countless examples of outstanding canines; their instinctive loyalty and dedication make them capable of astonishing, often lifesaving, feats. Here are just some of them:

RECORD DOGS

• Smallest domestic dog: A Yorkshire Terrier from Britain measured 3¼ in (9.5 cm) from nose to root of tail and stood 2½ in (63 cm) at the shoulder when it died aged nearly two in 1945.

• Largest domestic dog: An Old English Mastiff named Zorba stood 37 in (94 cm) and weighed 343 lb (155.558 kg) in 1989.

• Oldest domestic dog: An Australian Cattle Dog named Bluey was 29 years, five months when he was euthanized in 1939.

BLUEY

COURAGEOUS DOGS

ROY

• In Sweden in 1977, a pet German Shepherd, Roy, rescued a toddler from a narrow 36-ft (11-m) high ledge. Sensing the nature of the danger, he crept along on his belly, seized the child's diaper in his jaws, and shuffled back to the window.

• Sheepdog Nipper saved 300 ewes stuck in a burning barn on a British farm. When human rescue attempts failed, he battled tirelessly until he had led most of the animals out. He was awarded a medal by PRO-Dogs for his courage.

HELPFUL DOGS

• Formal dog training began in 1916 in Germany, to help those blinded during World War I. Soon after, in Switzerland, Dorothy Eustis trained a German Shepherd, Kiss (later Buddy) to be the first guide dog.

GUIDE DOG

• Cocker Spaniel Lucy answers the telephone for her deaf owner. She was trained by Hearing Dogs for the Deaf, a charity founded in 1982 by deaf actress Elizabeth Quinn, star of *Children of a Lesser God*.

DEVOTED DOGS

HACHIKO

• A small bronze statue at Shibuya station, Japan, commemorates Hachiko. This Akita dog accompanied his master, Dr. Ueno, to the station every day and was there at night to greet him on his return. After Dr. Ueno died in 1925, Hachiko waited daily for ten years until his own death.

• In 1923 a part-collie dog, Bobbie, walked 3,100 miles (5,000 km) to reach his Oregon home after losing his owner while on vacation in Indiana. It took him six months, but he managed to cross cities, large rivers, and the formidable Rocky Mountains.

DOG FEATS

• In the winter of 1925, when bad weather made flying impossible, over 100 sled dogs covered 1,086 km (675 miles) of Alaskan wilderness to deliver antitoxin serum to Nome, a town in the grip of a diphtheria epidemic. Headed by Balto, the sled team took five days to tackle the -60°F (-50.4°C) temperatures, blizzards, and freezing rivers. The journey is relived each year in the Iditarod Trail Race.

BALTO

• Barry, the most famous St. Bernard rescue dog, is said to have saved the lives of more than 40 people when he worked at the Hospice du Grand St. Bernard from 1800 to 1812.

WAR DOGS

• During World War 1, dogs were trained to carry messages, find injured soldiers on the battlefield, and transport Red Cross medical supplies.

RED CROSS DOG

• In 1918 Airedale Jack, saved a whole battalion by carrying a vital message across a savage fusillade. Badly wounded by shrapnel he covered his last 1.6 miles (3 km) unable to walk properly. Once he had delivered the message, he died. Airedale Jack received a posthumous Victoria Cross for his gallantry.

• Mongrel Rip was found homeless after an air raid in London, 1940. He went on to sniff out many casualties during heavy bombing.

Resources

Many organizations exist to fulfill the various needs of dog owners. If you have a purebred dog and would like to explore breed-specific issues with other owners, ask your veterinarian, or the person from whom you obtained your dog, about a breed club you can contact. There are too many breed clubs to list here.

The organizations shown here focus on issues of general concern in the areas of animal health, welfare, showing, training, or rescue. A sampling of publications relevant to dog owners is also provided. When contacting any of these organizations for information, it may bring a quicker reply if you include a stamped, self-addressed envelope.

AGAINST CRUELTY

American Humane Association
63 Inverness Drive East
Englewood, CO 80112
(866) 242-1877

American Society for the Prevention of Cruelty to Animals (ASPCA)
424 East 92nd Street
New York, NY 10128
(212) 876-7700

Humane Society of the United States
2100 L Street, NW
Washington, DC 20037
(202) 452-1100

People for the Ethical Treatment of Animals (PETA)
PO Box 42516
Washington, DC 20015
(301) 770-PETA

DOG HEALTH

American Holistic Vet Medical Association
2214 Old Emmorton Rd.
Bel Air, MD 21015
(410) 569-0795

American Veterinary Medical Association
1931 North Meacham Rd.
Schaumburg, IL 60173
(847) 925-8070

Animal Medical Center
510 East 62nd Street
New York, NY 10021
(212) 838-8100

Feline and Canine Friends
505 N. Bush Street
Anaheim, CA 92805
(714) 635-7975

HUMAN–DOG BOND

Assistance Dog Institute
PO Box 2334
Rohnert Park, CA 94927
(707) 585-0300

Delta Society
580 Naches Ave. SW
Renton, WA 98055
(425) 226-7357

**National Education for
Assistance Dog Services
(NEADS)**
PO Box 213
West Boylston, MA 01583
(508) 422-9064

The Seeing Eye, Inc.
PO Box 375
Morristown, NJ 07963
(973) 539-4425

SHOW BODIES

**The American Kennel
Club (AKC)**
260 Madison Avenue
New York, NY 10016
(212) 696-8200

United Kennel Club
100 East Kilgore Road
Kalamazoo, MI 49002
(269) 343-9020

DOG PUBLICATIONS

Animal Times
PO Box 42516
Washington, DC 20015
(301) 770-PETA

ASPCA Animal Watch
424 East 92nd Street
New York, NY 10128
(212) 876-7700

Bloodlines
United Kennel Club, Inc.
100 East Kilgore Road
Kalamazoo, MI 49001
(616) 343-9020

The Canine Chronicle
4727 NW 80th Ave.
Ocala, FL 34482
(352) 369-1104

Dog Fancy
Subscriptions Department
PO Box 53264
Boulder, CO 80322
(800) 365-4421

Dog News
1115 Broadway
New York, NY 10010
(212) 462-9588

Dog World Magazine
3 Burroughs
Irvine, CA 92618
(949) 855-8822

**Purebred Dogs/American
Kennel Gazette**
American Kennel Club
260 Madison Avenue
New York, NY 10016
(212) 696-8200

Showsight Magazine
8848 Beverly Hills
Lakeland, FL 33809
(863) 858-3839

Glossary

BAITING
The setting of dogs upon other animals for sport.

BAY
The deep howl of a hound on a trail.

BREED
A group of animals within a species whose traits are transmitted from generation to generation.

CANID
A member of the dog family.

CANINE
Of or like a dog.

CARNIVORE
A flesh-eating animal.

CONGENITAL DEFECT
Abnormality arising as a result of breeding. It is not necessarily hereditary.

CORDED COAT
Coat that has ropelike twists of hair formed from intertwined topcoat and undercoat.

COURSING
Hunting that relies on sight rather than scent.

CROP
Cutting off all or part of the ears for cosmetic or medical reasons.

CROSSBRED
Produced as a result of crossbreeding, particularly of two pure breeds.

CROSSBREED
The offspring of parents of two or more breeds.

CULOTTE
Long hair on thighs and forelegs.

DEWCLAW
A nonfuntional claw on the inside of the leg.

DEWLAP
Loose, pendulous skin under the throat.

DOCKING
Cutting off all or part of the tail for cosmetic or medical reasons.

DRAFT ANIMAL
An animal that pulls a load.

EXTINCT
When a species or breed ceases to exist.

FEATHERING
A long fringe of hair on ears, legs, tail, or body.

FERAL
A once-domestic animal that has reverted to the wild.

FIELD TRIALS
Contests between gundogs to test their proficiency.

FLEWS
The fleshy, hanging upper lips of a dog.

GENES
Units that carry hereditary characteristics from parents to offspring.

GLANDS
Organs that secrete chemicals for the body to use.

GUARD HAIRS
The long, heavy hairs of the topcoat.

HEAT
The period in which a bitch ovulates and looks for a mate.

HEIGHT
Distance from a dog's withers to the ground.

HORMONES
Chemical "messages," produced by glands that travel through blood.

INTERBREEDING
Breeding between two breeds or species.
MONGREL
A crossbreed. Sometimes called a random-bred dog.
MOLT
The (usually) seasonal shedding of the coat.
MUZZLE
The foreface; the head in front of the eyes. A guard over a dog's jaws to stop it from biting.
MUTATION
A genetic change that can be either harmless or unhealthy.
NATURAL SELECTION
The breeding of animals without human interference.
NEUTER
To remove an animal's reproductive organs.
OMNIVOROUS
An animal that feeds on all types of food.
OVULATION
Production of eggs in a female animal.
PEDIGREE
The record of a dog's ancestry.
PREDATOR
A carnivorous animal.

PRICK EARS
Erect, pointed ears.
PRIMITIVE
Of an early stage of development.
PUREBRED
An animal whose parents are of the same breed.
RATTER
A dog that catches and kills rats.
RETRACTABLE CLAWS
Claws that can be sheathed when not in use (as in cats).
SCAVENGER
An animal that feeds on discarded or decaying matter.
SCENT HOUND
A hound that hunts by ground scent.
SELECTIVE BREEDING
Breeding of animals by humans in order to achieve desired features.
SIGHT HOUND
A dog that hunts more by sight than scent.
SPECIES
A group of animals or plants that have certain common characteristics. These differentiate it from other groups.

STOP
The dip before a dog's eyes between skull and muzzle.
STRIP
In grooming, to remove old hair from a (usually) long coat.
TICKING
A fur color distinguished by bands of color on each hair.
TOPCOAT
Heavy, primary, or guard hair.
TOPKNOT
Wavy hair on the top of the head.
TRACK
To follow the trail of animal or person.
TRICOLOR
Three-colored – often black, white, and tan.
UNDERCOAT
The dense, usually short and soft coat closest to the skin.
UNDERSHOT JAW
A jaw in which the lower front teeth protrude beyond the upper front teeth.
WITHERS
The highest point on the body just behind the neck.

Index